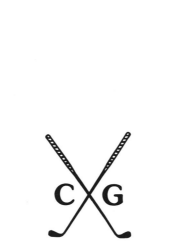

## THE CLASSICS OF GOLF

*Edition of*

# *GOLFERS' GOLD*

*by*

# *Tony Lema*

## *with Gwilym S. Brown*

*Foreword by Herbert Warren Wind*
*Afterword by Dave Anderson*

*ISBN 0-940889-17-X*

# Foreword

*In every decade, the golfers who are coming onto their games and the sportswriters who are coming of age discover "the tour", that long, exhausting swing of weekly tournaments which crosses the country from California to Florida during the winter and then, pausing every so often for a major event—the Masters in April, the United States Open in June, the British Open in July, and the P.G.A. Championship in August—winds its way into North and South Carolina, Louisiana, Texas for weeks, Nevada, Ohio, Maryland, New York, and Connecticut, up into Canada, back into Virginia, Illinois, Michigan, Tennessee, Colorado, Massachusetts again, and Wisconsin, until, with the coming of autumn, football, and brisker days, it heads back to the warm-weather states again. A great deal has been written about the tour—its official name now is the PGA Tour—from the era of Walter Hagen, Gene Sarazen, and Leo Diegel in the 1920s, through the emergence of Byron Nelson, Sam Snead, and Ben Hogan in the late 1930s, the period in the 1960s when Arnold Palmer, Gary Player, and Jack Nicklaus brought so much excitement to golf, and the very international golf scene we have today in this era of Seve Ballesteros, Tom Watson, Bernhard Langer, Fuzzy Zoeller, Greg Norman, Tze-Chung Chen, and Sandy Lyle. In my judgment, the book that captures life on the tour better than all the others is "Golfers' Gold", which was written by Tony Lema and Gwilym S. Brown in 1964. In the years it covers, Palmer, Nicklaus, and Player were regular members of the caravan, as were Julius Boros, Ken Venturi, Mike Souchak, Dow Finsterwald, Billy Casper, Tommy Bolt, Gene Littler, Doug Sanders, Bob Rosburg, Doug Ford, Paul Harney, Raymond Floyd, Frank Stranahan, Cary Middlecoff, Bo Wininger, Jerry Barber, Johnny Palmer, Jay and Lionel Hebert, Shelley Mayfield, Jimmy Demaret, Sam Snead, Dick Mayer, Al Besselink, Jim Ferree, Johnny Pott, Tommy Jacobs, Jackie Burke, Don January, Art Wall, Bobby Nichols, Fred Hawkins, Billy Maxwell, Chick Harbert, Don Fairfield, Phil Rodgers, Don Whitt, Mason Rudolph, Ernie Vossler, Dave Hill, Bob Goalby, Bill Collins, Pete Cooper, Gay Brewer, Tommy Aaron, Dan Sikes, Bob Charles, Bruce Devlin,*

*Walker Inman, Jacky Cupit, Bruce Crampton, Dave Ragan, Ted Kroll, and a few other fellows who could also hit the ball. They are all part of the fabric of this book.*

*When I read "Golfers' Gold" soon after it came out, I thought it was one of the best golf books I'd ever read. When I re-read it recently, it seemed a far greater achievement. I was bowled over by the thoroughness with which it covers every facet of life on the tour, and by the way it constantly keeps revving itself up in order to present the clearest, wryest, and most honest possible picture of what the tour was like in the last half of the 1950s and the first half of the 1960s when Anthony David Lema became a regular on it after spending a year as the head pro of a nine-hole municipal course in Elko, Nevada. "Golfers' Gold" takes him through 1963, when Lema really established himself as an outstanding player by winning the Memphis Open, being at the heart of the action in both the Masters and the U.S. Open, and playing a prominent role in the victory of our Ryder Cup team. Success turned Lema's head just right. After winning fourteen thousand dollars by finishing a stroke behind Nicklaus in the 1963 Masters, he decided to delay no further and marry his fiancée, Betty Cline, an American Airlines stewardess he had met in 1961. Two weeks later they were married in San Francisco.*

*Lema and Brown have a good story to tell. Lema's father died when he was three, and his mother had to raise a family of three boys and one girl in the industrial section of Oakland, California. Lema is extremely forthright in recalling his early years: "I was very tough to handle in high school, ran with a rough crowd, and though we got in trouble quite a bit we were lucky enough to stay out of the local lockup . . . We got in trouble because we would sit around and booze it up from time to time, then start talking big and pump ourselves up with false courage. Phew! Talk about your close calls. Thank goodness for golf." (The entire book possesses a basic candor.) When Lema was twelve, he started to caddy at the Lake Chabot municipal course. He began to play golf in his early teens, and quickly fell in love with it. Unlike team games, golf poses a strong, individual challenge to each aspiring player. It didn't take Lema long to become a good golfer. During his high-school years, he was so smitten with the game that he often played hooky from school.*

*During his summer vacations, he arranged to work on the nightshift at one of the local canneries so that he could play golf during the day. A good many fellows with Tony's orientation toward golf learn in their high-school days about the colleges that offer golf scholarships to promising young players. Somehow or another, this information never reached him. He had a good mind and he would have undoubtedly got a lot more out of college than most golfers on scholarships do. They are inclined to look upon college as a prep school for the pro tour. Not knowing exactly what to do after high school, Lema joined the Marines. The fighting was over before he was sent to Korea. He served there as an observer in the artillery corps. On his return to this country, Lema, still in uniform, gravitated to golf again. He played in the All-Marine Championship at Parris Island, South Carolina, and in the All-Service Championship at Langley Air Force Base, in Virginia.*

*When his hitch in the Marine Corps was up, Lema drove home to Oakland. He was on the highway east of San Francisco listening to some music on the radio when he heard the wail of a police siren behind him. He pulled over to the side of the road, all too conscious of what a wrenching way this was to return to civilian life. The police officer turned out to be an old golfing friend from Oakland. "We lit up cigarettes and talked a little bit there by the side of the road," Lema relates. "When he had heard that my plans for the future seemed to stretch no further than a stamping machine at the Gerber Food cannery in Oakland, he told me that the San Francisco Golf Club was interviewing applicants for a spot as an assistant on its professional staff and that I should try to get the job. I went right over."*

*This anecdote seemed to come right off the page when I read it, it was that graphic and it was a patently critical moment in Lema's life. What extraordinary good fortune! There are many other passages in "Golfers' Gold" that are related with such sensibility that the reader shares the dramatic moments that Lema and his friends in golf experience on and off the tour. This is testimony to the rare quality of the collaboration of Lema and Brown. Both men not only brought talent to the book but they also gave it the requisite time, patience, and discipline that distinguishes superior books.*

*Of course, it doesn't hurt "Golfers' Gold" that the story it tells* is about the adventurous, up-and-down, Dickensian route that Tony Lema travelled as he moved from his post as assistant professional at the San Francisco Golf Club in 1955 to his maturing in 1963 into a shining star of the P.G.A. tour. Along the way, Lema learned a lot about golf and a lot about life. He spent his first full year on the tour in 1958. He had an exceedingly promising rookie year, and he also acquitted himself well in 1959. The next two years, he suffered through a melange of attitudinal and technical problems, and his golf game disappeared. A lot of people contributed to Lema's eventual straightening out his thinking and his shotmaking. One time when he was in Detroit, for instance, he called Horton Smith on the phone. Horton told him to come on over to the Detroit Golf Club, and he gave Lema a lesson in putting that cured his troubles on the green for good. He got a lot of help from his tour caddie, Wally Heron—"he is fifty-five, gray-haired, and always presents a neat, well-pressed exterior". Wally could sense when Lema was on the verge of losing his self-control, and could settle him down. The interest and advice of a number of the touring pros was not lost on Lema. For all these reasons and others, he was able to get it all together in the autumn of 1962, and his play on the tour that autumn earned him an invitation to the 1963 Masters. He played beautifully at Augusta National. He holed a long birdie putt on the seventy-second green, which gave him a 70 for the round and a four-round total of 287. In order to beat him, Jack Nicklaus had to par the last two holes, which he did. The confidence that Lema gained was evident from then on both in tour tournaments and in the major championships. He had a good shot at winning the 1963 U.S. Open at The Country Club in Brookline, Massachusetts, and ended up two shots behind the three men who tied for first: Boros, the eventual winner, Palmer, and Cupit.

"Golfers' Gold" carries the rise of Lema through the 1963 season and presages the golden years that lay ahead for him. In 1964, he had by far the best year of his career. He won the Crosby, the Thunderbird Open, the Buick Open, and the Cleveland Open. On top of this, he won the British Open, his first major title, at St. Andrews. Rounds of 73 and 68 on the first two days gave him a nine-stroke lead on Nicklaus. On the final day, Lema started the first of his two rounds an hour and a half after

*Nicklaus had teed off. They passed each other when Nicklaus was playing the fourteenth and Lema the sixth. Jack was five under par for his round at that point, and Lema was three over after the first five holes. Nicklaus, at that moment, had picked up eight strokes on Lema. Jack went on to finish that round in 66, but Lema reacted to this challenge by making birdies on the seventh, ninth, tenth, fourteenth, fifteenth, and eighteenth holes for a 68. In the afternoon, Nicklaus shot a 68, a terrific round in the high winds, but Lema, playing superbly, finished with a 70. This gave him a winning total of 279, five strokes lower than the total of the nearest man, Nicklaus.*

*In 1965, Lema had another productive season. He won the Buick and Cleveland Opens. He made a fine defense of his British Open title, tying for fifth place at Birkdale. He was on our Ryder Cup team that year, and was a primary force in the American victory at Birkdale. On the first day, he was teamed with Boros in the foursomes. In the morning, they defeated Lionel Platts and Peter Butler, 1 up, and in the afternoon they defeated Jimmy Martin and Jimmy Hitchcock, 5 and 4. The next day, when the teams played four-ball matches, Boros and Lema Lost to Neil Coles and Bernard Hunt, 1 down, in the morning. In the afternoon, when Lema was partnered with Venturi, they beat Coles and Hunt, 1 up. On the third day, Lema won both of his singles. He defeated Butler, 1 up, in the morning, and Christy O'Connor, 6 and 4, in the afternoon.*

*In 1966, Lema's last year, he won the Oklahoma City Open. As most golfers remember, shortly after returning to this country after playing in the British Open at Muirfield, Lema and his wife were killed when the private plane in which they were traveling crashed on landing at Lansing, Illinois, on June 24, 1966. One of the many heart-felt tributes to Tony Lema was that by Jack Nicklaus: "It would have been historically wrong if an accomplished golfer like Tony had not won a major championship. His victory in the 1964 British Open assures him of being remembered for all time. . . Indeed, when he was playing his best, he had a greater sense of artistry than any of his contemporaries."*

*The other half of this outstanding collaboration, Gwilym Slater Brown, was born in 1928. (Gwilym is the Welsh form of William.) After attending Manuit boarding school, near Pawl-*

ing, N.Y., and the Cambridge School, he entered Harvard in 1947. He was president of his house, Leverett House, and graduated in 1951. I got to know Gwil in 1954 when we were both on the staff of the newly founded weekly magazine, Sports Illustrated. A tall, good-looking, enthusiastic fellow who played all games well and had a true love of sports, he proved to be a valuable member of the magazine. He could do anything. He wrote some wonderful studies of track-and-field stars, helped no end by his own infatuation, long before the vogue for jogging, with long-distance runs on the back roads in the countryside near Pawling, where he, his wife Joyce, and their children spent their weekends. He wrote many fine golf articles. I remember a brilliant instruction piece on putting which he did with Billy Casper, one of the premier putters of our time. I would guess that the years with Sports Illustrated that Gwil enjoyed the most were those from 1967 to 1970 when he was the magazine's representative at Time, Inc.'s London office. I remember well the Publisher's Memo that included a photograph of Our Man in London walking happily down Bond Street carrying his brief-case.

Gwil Brown had a faculty for friendship. We were part of a group who for a decade went to the New York Giants football games at Yankee Stadium. We played a lot of enjoyable golf and got together at many of the tournaments. I remember with particular clarity the 1963 British Open at Lytham St. Annes. At the end of seventy-two holes, Bob Charles, of New Zealand, and Phil Rodgers, of the United States, were tied. They met the next day in a 36-hole playoff—the last 36-hole playoff in history. As the only two Americans still on hand at the championship, it fell to us to take care of Rodgers, an exceedingly ebullient fellow in those days. The evening before the playoff, he put away two complete dinners. He was in good form in the playoff, but Charles, an extraordinary putter, must have holed at least a dozen putts between fifteen and fifty feet on the undulating greens. One of them, a thirty-five foot sidehiller for a birdie on the eighth hole in the afternoon, came only moments after Rodgers had holed a forty-five-foot downhiller for a birdie, and Charles' covering putt just about settled matters.

Gwil put a tremendous amount of work into his book with Lema. I believe their friendship started in 1961 when Gwil did *a story on the American professionals who were playing the Caribbean tour. "Golfers' Gold" was a great success, but Gwil's work for* Sports Illustrated *gave him little time to take on further outside writing. He died in 1974 from a disease from which there was no chance of recovery. He was a wonderful fellow.*

*Herbert Warren Wind*

# Golfers' Gold

## An Inside View of the Pro Tour

### by Tony Lema with Gwilym S. Brown

**Little, Brown and Company · Boston · Toronto**

*with photos*

Some of the material in this book
originally appeared in *Sports Illustrated*.

*Published simultaneously in Canada*
*by Little, Brown & Company (Canada) Limited*

PRINTED IN THE UNITED STATES OF AMERICA

# Contents

# *Illustrations*

# *Golfers' Gold*

# 1 / The tour — an explosive decade

THIS is a story about the Pro Tour. Also known as the Professional Golfers' Association of America Tournament Circuit, or Pro Golf's Circuitous Caravan, or The Long Gray Grind for Gold, or, quite simply, as The Tour.

It is also a story about one of The Tour's most interesting performers. That's me, the narrator. Also known as Anthony David Lema, or Champagne Tony, or, quite simply, as Tony.

There are perhaps a hundred touring pros like me — or near enough like me to make my story their story. We float along on a tournament schedule that runs from year end to year end. We compete for almost $2,500,000 in prize money and hundreds of thousands of dollars in peripheral income. This is a great deal of money and some professional golfers get very rich. Unfortunately it is not nearly enough to go around, to support all the players who chase after this kind of wealth. Some professional golfers get very broke. We are migrant sportsmen moving from state to state, from city to city, from country club to country club, and many of the millions of people who watch us think, "Gosh, what a ball. Playing a game for all that money; traveling all over the U.S. and all over the world!"

Well, the tour is a ball — some of the time. The money is there — if you are good enough to win it. And as for the traveling? Listen to what my friend Don Whitt, who has been on the tour since 1955, once remarked.

"I guess I've traveled a hundred thousand miles a year on the pro tour," he said while lying on his back in a San Juan hotel room, too tired to go to the beach, "but the only thing of interest I've ever seen is the Washington Monument."

That is a complaint, but it is also nothing more than a statement of fact. We are not out here on the tour to sightsee. We are out here to make our living. To some the tour proves too tough a way to make a living and so they abandon it. Others of us stick with it until one day we suddenly reach that moment of fulfillment when we know that we have chosen the right profession. We have finally reached a point in life from which we can walk forward with a sense of pride and of accomplishment, a moment that has torn from us years of self-doubt and has replaced these with a confidence that is almost ecstatic.

The tour has had me on it full-time since 1958. While it has grown steadily during those years, I have skidded up and down it like a mountain goat. In 1959, as I was about to begin my second year on the tour, I had every reason to believe that I might eventually become what Arnold Palmer *has* become. By 1961, after two extraordinarily dismal years of competitive golf, I was nothing more than an exhausted swimmer struggling to keep from being sucked down by an undertow of failure. Then suddenly in 1962 I bobbed up to the surface once again like a cork; and in 1963 — wow! Champagne Tony, the Terror of the Tour, the playboy's playboy. Now? Well, now I'm just Tony Lema again. One of the best, capable of being *the* best, but also in danger of drifting out of sight.

The first moment at which I could begin to feel that there was a purpose behind my career as a touring pro did not come until October 28, 1962, as I stood on the edge of the third green at the Mesa Verde Country Club in Costa Mesa, California. I was twenty-eight years old and my fifth year on the tour was just ending. I had won some lesser tournaments, including the Mexican Open, but though I had played in 180 of them I had never won what is described as an Official PGA Event — meaning one of the big ones.

Now I watched as one of the tour's leading winners and leading players, Bob Rosburg, crouched over a putt of about 10 feet. Rosburg and I had tied for first after 72 holes of the Orange County Open and were then sent out again for a sudden death play-off. The first player to win a hole wins the tournament. We had played even through the first two extra holes. On the third hole, 170 yards long and reachable from the tee with a 5-iron, we had both hit good shots close to the flagstick and I had then stroked in my putt of 10½ feet. Now, as I watched, my tension was so great that I could not stand still. If he missed his putt I would win my first official tournament. I held my putter in one hand and my ball in the other and fidgeted, barely able to breathe. Rosburg hit his putt. It was a good one, rolling straight at the hole. It hit the back of the cup, popped into the air and came down on solid ground. He had missed. I could hardly believe it. I have no memory of doing it, but the feeling of relief and exhilaration was so great that I leaped high in the air and flung my golf ball almost all the way back to the tee.

Times like this make life on the pro tour worthwhile, all right, but they don't come very often. For me the events that took place on that warm October afternoon were the climax of the seven eventful years in my life as a professional golfer. These were important years, not just for me, but in the history of the pro golf tour itself. My own personal story, a small but revealing part of the story of the tour, begins

with my pre-tour years of 1956 and 1957, when I worked
obscurely as a club professional. It continues with my successful, if not sensational, rookie year on the circuit in 1958,
when tournament golf was just starting to become the sporting giant it is today. That year I played well, made some
money, made friends, and came heartbreakingly close to winning a couple of tournaments. This was a year that seemed
bursting with a promise of future glory. I followed it, however, not with a series of spectacular victories, but with the
horrible years of 1959 and 1960, when my game and my
usually happy frame of mind collapsed like a paper tent in a
downpour; when I moved like a zombie from city to city,
when there was not enough booze or enough women in
the whole United States to cheer me up, though I certainly
tried to exhaust the supply. I hated professional golf and
hated myself. Suddenly, just when I had determined to quit
the tour completely, came the encouraging year of 1961. My
game came back, my morale came back, and parties and girls
were fun again, not just a way of forgetting how miserable I
was. This time the promise was fulfilled. The next year, 1962,
was a year of real success and one that led directly into the
at least modest fame and fortune that came with 1963. In '63
I won tournaments and I made a lot of money. I was honored
by being named to the Ryder Cup team, which is to professional golf what making an Olympic team is to amateur sports,
and I found a lovely wife. I am not about to claim that I am
the biggest man in my business — that title still belongs to
players like Arnold Palmer and Jack Nicklaus; and no one out
here on the tour can ever predict what his future will be. But
up to now my story has been a success story in the purest
American tradition, and I thank God that I have been fortunate enough to have had it happen to me.

[ 6 ]

## The tour — an explosive decade

When a man on the tour is winning tournaments, every day seems like a ticker-tape parade up Fifth Avenue. The crowds cheer every shot, you're on TV and in the newspapers everywhere you go. The money is coming in so fast you don't know what to do with it and the pretty girls are swarming around like honeybees. Playing golf seems as effortless as reading in a hammock.

Fortunately or unfortunately, depending on how well you're doing it, playing golf is only half the story of making a success of the pro tour. Arnold Palmer with his corporations and his world tours isn't the only player faced with the task of holding his competitive edge against a constant riptide of distractions. A sound swing isn't the miracle ingredient. Survival depends a great deal on toughness of mind and spirit. Yet there is no way of teaching survival for our extraordinary life. Like walking, it is something each man must learn as he stumbles along. I would say that the most successful, best-rounded touring pro must be part athlete, salesman, public relations expert, certified public accountant and — perhaps most important of all — very much a showman. We have no director, no rehearsed lines to say, and our stage covers a hundred and fifty acres, but we are showmen just as much as Danny Kaye is a showman, or Bob Hope or Frank Sinatra. My half dozen years on the pro tour have thrown me in with rowdy Texas oilmen, agile-minded industrial big shots, suave supersalesmen, millionaires, show people and playboys, but I've met very few people who lead a life anywhere near as strange as ours. Yet while being so much apart from life in the United States, it is also very much a part of it. This is such a confusing contrast that we start every explanation about our hectic, nomadic existence by saying, "Well, out here on the tour . . ."

[ 7 ]

In many ways life "out here on the tour" is like a long, risky trip into orbit. Yet tournament competition is so gripping, gets so deep into a player's blood, that those who are on it love it, those who have left it itch to get back. The tour is crowded with players who should have left it years ago and with players who never should have come out on it. But where else can a man advance on pure and simple ability? Where only scores, not friends in the right places or office politics, count? What sport can yield an annual income of $500,000 to a man of thirty-four — like Arnold Palmer? Or an annual income of $300,000 to a man of twenty-four — like Jack Nicklaus? Or an income of $100,000 to a former San Francisco cannery worker of thirty — like me — who would probably be back there at a stamping machine right now if it weren't for the pro golf tour?

How do you prepare a man for this kind of career? College can't do it. Working in a cannery certainly can't do it. A good teaching professional can teach a young man to hit a golf ball with a stick pretty near perfectly every time, but how do you teach that man to hit that tiny ball with a long, whippy stick when fifteen thousand people are jammed around him like a crowd at a six-alarm fire, when several million eyes are peering at him on television, and when $250,000 is riding, directly or indirectly, on the next shot he hits? Well, some of us, obviously, have learned to do it. Even a highly strung choke artist like myself has learned to do it. Those of us who have managed to float on top of the rough current of the pro tour and learned to take the fantastic pressure of playing for high stakes have learned to do it by doing it. We have learned as we went along, and this book, I hope, will make clear some of the lessons that we took far from the practice tee.

As complex as it may seem today, the pro tour is something

[ 8 ]

that has evolved quite naturally in the United States during this century. Back in the 1920's there may have been perhaps a dozen tournaments during the course of the year, played at widely scattered times in widely scattered places. There was not the tightly organized circuit we now know. Eventually golf promoters like Bob Harlow and Fred Corcoran persuaded various groups — Chambers of Commerce, charities, resorts, and even private businesses — to sponsor a greater number of events. They more or less organized what was then a fairly small group of players into a troupe that competed on a fairly regular basis. By World War II, though the tour was much smaller in size than it is today, the groundwork had been thoroughly done.

After the war the tour, under the sponsorship of the Professional Golfers' Association and the various groups around the country who were interested in putting up the cash to back events, expanded until in the early 1950's there were about thirty-five stops a year and about fifty regulars performing at them. Then, for a variety of reasons, golf really caught on.

The result is that the face of tournament golf has changed drastically in just the last ten years; and not only because in 1953 a great many of the players traveled by trailer (Palmer, Gene Littler and a great many others started that way), while now they go by jet. Up until that time there existed almost a set pattern by which a young player would break into professional golf and subsequently into professional tournament golf. As a kid he would caddy. As he got older, provided he had chosen golf as his profession, he would most likely take a job as an assistant professional at a neighborhood club, working around the shop, selling merchandise, sweeping floors, repairing golf clubs and occasionally getting out on the course itself to practice and play. Eventually, if his game was a good one, he would compete in local tournaments as a warm-up to jumping out on the main tournament circuit. That's the way Walter Hagen and Gene Sarazen began their great careers as tournament golfers fifty years ago. Quite a bit later Byron Nelson, Ben Hogan and Sam Snead, to name just a few, climbed to golfing fame up the same thoroughly tested ladder.

Those days are now as dead as the Big Apple. First of all, golf has a much broader appeal today than it did even ten years ago. Our last two Presidents were good golfers. Filmed and live golf tournaments and matches of all sorts are always jumping out at viewers from the television picture tube. Secondly, as a direct result of this booming popularity, the professional tournament program has boomed too. There is so much money to be made in professional golf now that a great many college boys, who formerly would have been selling insurance, or stocks, or whatever, for a living, and unlimbering a once excellent golf swing only for an occasional round with a client, are out on the tour. And I don't just mean Jack Nicklaus. Every pro tournament is loaded with fine former college golfers who are almost completely unknown, but who hope to be able to work their way into the big money and can meanwhile make enough to keep going. A great many of these players have caddied, of course, as boys, but most of them have never seen the inside of a pro shop except as customers. Of the ten leading money earners in 1953 only one, Cary Middlecoff, had gone to college, while in 1963 eight of the ten leaders had.

The statistics alone are revealing. In 1953 the tournament pros played for a total of $625,000 in prize money. In 1963 that total reached over $2,200,000. In 1953 Lew Worsham was the leading money winner. He earned $34,000, but $25,000 of that sum came riding in on one shot, the famous wedge he holed out from 90 yards at the very last hole of George S. Mays's World Championship Golf. Doug Ford, who was just then beginning to make a name for himself and seems to go on forever without any loss in effectiveness, was second at $26,816. In tenth place that year was Tommy Bolt, who won $16,031.

These totals are insignificant by today's standards. It's almost the difference between shooting dice in a back-room crap game or playing at Monte Carlo. The leading money winner in 1963, Arnold Palmer, stuffed $128,000 into his bank account. In all modesty I must point out that the fourth-place man won twice what Worsham did ten years earlier; and the man tenth on the list, Bobby Nichols, won as much as leading money winner Worsham did in 1953. What golfer who can play a lick is going to want to sit in a back room polishing someone else's golf clubs if he can even nibble at this kind of money? What young amateur will be content to waste a smooth-as-silk golf swing selling an occasional life insurance policy when that same swing might bring in $100,000 a year playing tournament golf? The answer is, damned few.

The ladder that leads to the top of professional tournament golf today looks something like this. First of all, a great many golfers start very young, say between ten and twelve years of age. The family is probably a member of some club or other, or there are public courses in the area. The club or the town quite probably has a junior golf program, and by the time the boy is old enough for high school he not only has had plenty of competition, but also some pretty good teaching as well. By high school, therefore, he knows within reason just how good a golfer he can become.

The next step up the golfing ladder is an athletic scholarship to college, preferably one in the South or Southwest, where golf can be played all year round. This may seem surprising to many people, but golf has become so important a sport that dozens of colleges offer some form of free board, room and tuition to kids who can play it. Over two hundred colleges own golf courses. Four years of this kind of tough competition, and the young golfer will be practically as experienced as the most hardened touring pro. Many college players, like Houston's Jacky Cupit, Iowa's Jack Rule, Memphis State's Mason Rudolph, who had made a ripple but no resounding splash as amateurs, were so polished when they joined the tour that they were able to win tournaments almost immediately. Others, however, prefer to take a year's seasoning on the big-time amateur circuit. This is not only a great deal of fun, but it also gives the good players a chance to gain national recognition by winning an important amateur event or by making one of the international teams like the Walker Cup, to play against Great Britain; the Americas Cup, to play against Canada and Mexico; or the Eisenhower Cup, to play in the World Amateur Championship. I don't mean to say that every player on the tour today is a college man — far from it — but it is the established new trend. The point is that we have a great many professional players, trained in college to do other work, who are playing professionally because it has suddenly become both lucrative and exciting. By the same token, most of the professional golfers of ten or more years ago were playing because it was the only thing they knew.

A few of the old school are still playing pretty well on the tour, and it is significant that they all got on it at a relatively advanced age; they didn't have the experience that today's young golfers get so early. Had they joined the tour at twenty-one or so they would have been eaten alive by the Hogans, Nelsons and Sneads. Doug Ford, whose family name was Fortunato before they shortened it, is one. He is straight from the streets of New York and the fastest player on the tour. He often hits his shot before his fellow competitor's has landed. Doug's father and three uncles are all teaching pros, but Doug didn't come out on the tour as a regular until 1950, the year he turned twenty-eight. In those days the purses were so small that he was able to make more money as an amateur. In his amateur days Ford was seldom a loser when the bet was big. He played often and he won often. The United States Golf Association hinted, however, that the kind of money Doug was making playing golf hardly went hand-in-hand with his designation as an amateur, and so Ford turned pro quickly, before the USGA could remove his amateur status.

Tommy Bolt was a carpenter's apprentice from Haworth, Oklahoma, when he finally decided to go out on the tour. He tried it a couple of times, had to be refinanced a couple of times, and finally stayed as a regular in 1950. By that time he was thirty-one years old. He was thirty-nine when he won the U.S. Open in 1958.

Ed Furgol was another latecomer to the tour. Despite a crippled left arm, Ed figured in 1945 that he had become a good enough golfer to turn pro and compete professionally. Ed was raised in the mill section of upstate New York and was a proud and determined competitor when he turned pro at the age of twenty-eight.

"I was still just a raggedy-assed kid," he says, "and those guys on the tour gave me a pretty tough time. They must have thought it was pretty funny for a guy with an arm like mine to try to play golf at all, let alone for a living."

Even Julius Boros, who won the U.S. Open in 1952 and again in 1963, certainly an indication of tremendous golfing talent, couldn't make up his mind to play the tour professionally until 1950, the year he was thirty years old. That kind of procrastination would be unthinkable today, yet here were Ford, who won the PGA in 1955 and the Masters two years later, and three Open champions — Bolt, Furgol and Boros — starting out on the tour in their late twenties and early thirties. Compare this with the ages at which some of the current leading players took up tournament golf on a full-time basis. Arnold Palmer was twenty-four, Jack Nicklaus twenty-one, Bill Casper twenty-three, Dow Finsterwald twenty-two, Gene Littler twenty-four, Gary Player twenty-two and Doug Sanders twenty-three.

Being a professional in golf should not be confused with being a touring pro. The tour is just one phase of professional golf. Actually, all a person has to do to turn pro is send a letter to the United States Golf Association (the association of clubs in this country that regulates the rules and the sport) announcing his intention to accept money for playing, teaching or working in a golf shop. He doesn't need to have played in a professional tournament or even have a job. This does not qualify him for the tour, however.

Unfortunately a great many golfers think it does. A good example of what can happen in this respect was given to me by Jack Tuthill, a two-handicap amateur and the PGA's tournament coordinator. In 1962 Jack was attempting to qualify for the U.S. Open. About two thousand golfers file entries for this tournament; the USGA, which runs it, limits the field to *all* professionals and amateurs with handicaps of two or less. To help reduce the starting field of 150 players, qualifying rounds are held late each spring throughout the country. Jack attempted to qualify on Long Island, and in the 36-hole round was paired with a young professional who worked at a driving range. While they played this young pro spoke casually of his desire to come out and give the tour a whirl. What a whirl it would have been if he'd been allowed on it. Poor Jack never did qualify for that Open, but it might have had something to do with the way his fellow qualifier was playing. This so-called "professional," this would-be touring pro, turned in a score of 106 in the morning round and 112 in the afternoon. This was about seventy shots higher than the score necessary to make the grade, but it was hardly surprising, since the fellow had probably never played more than eight or nine rounds of golf in his life.

There are many golfers, like Jack Tuthill's playing partner, who seem to think that it is almost as easy to make a success of the tour as it is to turn professional. The pros are constantly confronted by country club members who are pretty fair golfers, have just had a couple of quick ones in the men's grill, and have decided maybe we aren't such hotshots after all.

"Boy, I thought you guys would really tear old Pareasy Golf Club apart during the Choker's Open," the member says, shaking his head. "I used to be a member over there and even though I played it only once a week I was always able to get around in 72 or 73. You pros were having trouble breaking 70."

Everyone of us on the tour hears this kind of thing at least twice monthly. It is a tribute to our great restraint that one of us isn't booked for manslaughter every other week, because hardly anything can make a touring pro hotter under the collar than this. Let me explain why.

First of all, Joe Club Member and Joe Touring Pro play two completely different courses, even though they both tread the same fairways and putt the same greens. The club member, more often than not, will make his good scores from the middle tees, while the tournament pros will be teeing off not only from the extreme rear of every tee, but also from tees that have been especially constructed for the tournament. This means that on the whole we are playing a course anywhere from 400 to 800 yards longer than the member plays.

This is not the only difference. There are others almost as important. If the cup is cut into the center of each green the course will be relatively easy. Very often the member will be playing "winter rules," or "preferred lies," meaning that he can roll the ball around in the fairway with his clubhead until his ball is sitting up fat and sassy, practically begging to be hit. A course has to be in pretty rotten condition before we are allowed this luxury. Playing preferred lies can make a difference of several strokes a round. Then there is the question of holing all putts. A professional in a tournament must hole every putt, no matter how short, or he is disqualified. There are no "gimmes" on the pro tour. As a result many of us miss putts that Joe Club Member's opponent in his friendly match has been conceding. A two-foot putt doesn't look so short when missing it can mean a tournament victory or several thousand dollars in prize money. This brings up another point, the question of what is at stake when you are playing. When the prize is a couple of drinks at the bar it isn't too difficult to turn in a good score for 18 holes every now and then. Try to be this consistent when a small fortune, or at the very least your living, is at stake.

Finally, there is the question of local knowledge. Where scoring is concerned this is probably the most important factor. We see newcomers on the tour who are out here because they were shooting out the lights on their own course. They were turning in scores in the 60's so often it made their heads swim with thoughts of acclaim in the newspaper headlines and money in the bank. What such a young amateur — just turned pro — fails to realize is that most of his good scores were a direct result of the fact that he knew every blade of grass on the course, every slight undulation on the putting green, how far he was from the flagstick from every point on the course. On the tour we play a different course every week. Not only are the courses stretched out so long that you are practically teeing off in the next town, but there is always a different texture of grass — soft, thick bent grass one week, thick-bladed, crisp Bermuda the next. We play over sandy fairways, muddy fairways, and hard dirt fairways; on big greens and little greens, hilly greens and flat greens, bumpy greens and smooth greens. One week we will play on a wind-swept golf course that has about as many trees as an airport runway, the next on a course that has as many ups and downs as a roller coaster, enough trees to start a lumber mill, and is choked with sand traps, creeks, ponds and bushes. Visualize the cast of a big, brassy, Broadway musical trying to put on their show on somebody's front lawn one night, in a barn the next, and on a big theater stage the next, and you get only a slightly exaggerated idea of what a touring pro has to put up with. Experience and adaptability count for a lot. One of the features of life on the tour is the endless coming and going of players who shoot in the 60's on their own course back home and can't break 80 out here.

Alex Redl is the head professional at one of the toughest courses we play on each year, the Firestone Country Club in Akron, Ohio. This is the site of the American Golf Classic and the World Series of Golf and was where the PGA Championship was played in 1960. In fact, the course was redesigned to make it a sufficient challenge on which to hold the

PGA Championship. It contains two ponds, about a hundred sand traps in the fairway or around the green, and every fairway is lined on one side or the other with a wide assortment of trees. It is also 7000 yards long, and head professional Redl is pretty proud of his tough course. In '62 while I was playing in the American Golf Classic, Redl was still snorting about one of the entrants in the previous year's Ohio Open, played at Firestone. This is strictly a tournament for local and Midwestern pros and amateur golfers. This entrant was a young man from Toledo who had been playing such great golf that a bunch of his friends and business associates had actually raised a big pot of money to get him started on the circuit. The first stop on his way was the Ohio Open, merely a warm-up for his Grand Entrance. Well, this poor fellow supplies a perfect example of how bad a good player can look when he strays too far from home. He shot the first two rounds in 89 and 94, 43 strokes over par, didn't even qualify for the last two rounds of the tournament, and was headed home practically before anyone knew he had arrived.

This kind of thing happens, but the Professional Golfers' Association, which administers the tournament circuit, tries to keep it to a minimum. The PGA requires that every professional who plays the tour on a regular basis first obtain an Approved Player's card. This is his certificate of eligibility. The PGA headquarters are in Palm Beach Gardens, Florida, but it has some thirty-four sectional offices throughout the country. To obtain an Approved Player's card a golfer must first apply to his local section. He must produce character references, testimony that his golf game is a good one, and proof that he can support himself on the tour for at least a few months even if he never picks up a prize money check the whole time.

Okay. So our hero has made a name for himself locally. He has shown that he has a good, sound golf game, capable of producing good scores even on the tour. He is of fine, upstanding character and he has even rounded up some friends, business associates, or a backer willing to pay his expenses on the tour for one or two years while he is getting established. He packs up his gear, hops in his car and roars out to the first tournament, fairly drooling with eagerness to pick up a nice fat check.

But wait, what's this? He arrives at the scene and finds that he has to play in a tournament just to get into the tournament. This is called pre-tournament qualifying, and works something like this. Most of the PGA tournaments have a starting field of 120 to 150 players. This sounds like a lot, but there are always more players than places to be filled. To keep the field at this size the PGA has worked out a qualifying system. The fifty leading money winners of the previous year are exempt from pre-tournament qualifying. So are all tournament winners of the preceding twelve months. So are all those who made the 36-hole cut-off the previous week. So are all past PGA, Masters and Open champions. It goes on and on like that. The result, especially in the winter, when the Northern golf clubs are closed and their professional staffs have poured out onto the tour, is that there are not too many free spots in each tournament. At the Los Angeles Open, held in early January and traditionally the new year's first tournament, there are some 350 players competing in the pre-event qualifying round for about thirty or thirty-five places. At the Crosby about eighty players compete in the pre-tournament qualifying round for about twenty spots. This is standard procedure all winter, through California, Arizona, across Texas, into Louisiana and Florida, only easing up somewhat in the spring, when a great many of the players return to their club jobs. I know of numerous players out on the tour who hardly ever play in a tournament. Every week they try to qualify and every week they fail. Then they move on to the next town and try to qualify there. They are on the tour just as much as the rest of us, but the regular players only run into them now and then, either on the practice tee or when they have been lucky enough to qualify. They are a sort of Ghost Squadron of the tournament circuit. The regulars never see them, but they have been traveling right along with us.

At the Insurance City Open last year I encountered one player on the practice tee whom I had been paired with in a tournament five months earlier. This was the first time I had seen him since.

"Hiya, Bob," I said. "You been off the tour for a vacation?"

"No," he answered. "I've been out here all the time, but this is only the sixth tournament I've been able to play in all year."

It is not unusual for a player to pick up the tour at Los Angeles in January and stick with it right to the end of the winter and yet play in nothing but the pre-tournament qualifying rounds. Many of these are good players, too. Take the case of Raymond Floyd. He is a husky young golfer in his early twenties, who shows plenty of promise. The 1963 season was his first on the tour. As tough as it is to win a tournament, Floyd was able to do it within three months. He won the St. Petersburg Open in March. The remarkable thing about Floyd, however, is that up until that time he had not won a dime. He had not even been able to qualify for three of the nine tournaments that had been played up to that time. On the tour there is also a bitter little fact of tournament life called, quite simply, "the cut." It is appropriately named, because its existence makes a lot of us want to draw a knife across our throats from time to time. It is an elimination that takes place halfway through each tournament. After 36 holes only the leading sixty players are allowed to continue; the rest are simply lopped off like so much blubber. Well, in the six tournaments Floyd had qualified to play in, he was able to survive the cut only once. By winning at St. Petersburg, Raymond Floyd suddenly and dramatically graduated from the Ghost Squadron, but this success and others like it guarantee that the squadron's ranks will always be kept full.

# 2 / *The exceptional tourists*

WHEN I see what Palmer, Nicklaus and Player have been able to earn — both on and off the golf course — and what I am just beginning to make, it is startling to think that professional tournament golf is undoubtedly just entering its boom period. Some of us are on television almost as often as Garry Moore. A big-name winner like Palmer is a modern King Midas. Everything he touches, drinks, smokes, wears, or drives can turn to gold. The hair tonic he thinks he needs, the cigarette he smokes, the soda pop he drinks, the ties, shorts, jackets, slacks and shoes he wears, the car he drives, the clubs he swings and the ball he hits are all juicy sources of income. All he has to do is testify, yes, that's what I put in my hair, smoke, drink, wear, drive, swing and hit. The idea is that what is good enough for Palmer will also be good enough for ten million golf-nutty Americans who will then rush out and smoke, drink, wear, drive, swing and hit the same thing.

It is logical for Palmer, who was a National Amateur champion, or for Nicklaus, who was second in the U.S. Open as a twenty-year-old amateur and won the National Amateur title twice, to think in terms of big, big money when they leave the amateur ranks and become professionals. Most of the rest of us, however, didn't think that way when we first came "out here." Money was important, of course, but many other aspects of the game also drew us. The challenge of competition, the traveling, the joy of being able to play the game we loved for our livelihood. This explains why the tour is loaded with players who seem about as likely candidates for a career in professional golf as Albert Schweitzer. Just picking at random some of the people who have turned pro over the last few years can be very revealing. Why does a millionaire like Frank Stranahan turn pro? Or a business executive like Billy Booe? Or a former major league baseball star like Gerry Priddy? Or a current pro football star like John Brodie? Or a popular singer like Don Cherry? Or a licensed attorney like Dan Sikes? For money? Partly. But money is only a small part of the story with these people.

Muscular Frank Stranahan created quite a bit of excited babble when he announced back in 1955 that henceforth he was abandoning the ranks of those who play golf for fun alone. Frank comes from Toledo, Ohio, and is one of the heirs to the Champion Spark Plug business and fortune. As an amateur he had always been a terrific golfer. He won the British Amateur in 1948 and 1950, was on three Walker Cup teams, and had even won four important PGA circuit tournaments while still an amateur. What prompted Frank's decision to turn pro was that he was already playing in a great number of tournaments each year, as many as a good portion of the pros who were doing it for a living.

"It isn't fair to the rest of the amateurs," he explained, "for me to remain an amateur and still play as much as I do. I want to go out and test my game on a full-time basis against the best."

This made sense. What didn't make sense was that Frank went in for the whole turning pro bit. For a sum that must have seemed like cigar money he signed on with the Mac-Gregor sporting goods company, agreeing to play their clubs and their golf ball. Then, a short time later, for what I understand was a modest plot of Florida real estate, he was billing himself when he registered for a golf tournament as Frank Stranahan, Crystal River, Florida. The only thing you could figure from all this was that Frank was just trying to be one of the boys.

Trying to imagine Frank as just one of the boys can sometimes be pretty hard. He's a remarkable fellow in too many ways. Some years ago he decided that building up his body would help build up his golf game, so he took up weight lifting. The result now is a build — trim waist, big chest, broad shoulders, massive arms — that makes him look like Steve Reeves. He is such a good weight lifter, in fact, that in his early days on the tour he was able to win regional Amateur Athletic Union weight-lifting championships as he toured the country playing golf. He also traveled with a wardrobe that sometimes looked big enough to fill the main floor at Brooks Brothers. There is a story, possibly fictional, that one year Frank's car, a long black Cadillac, was stolen while he was playing in a golf tournament. The following day the state police discovered the car abandoned by the side of a road. They got in touch with Frank at the club and assured him his vehicle was safe and undamaged. "Never mind about the car," Frank shouted over the phone. "How about my clothes?"

Frank's a fine guy, and even though he plays the tour irregularly now — he is taking more of an interest in the family business — is still a pretty good golfer. But just in case anyone might still mistake him for just one of the boys, Frank turns up for tournaments from time to time with a valet.

During his years on the pro tour Frank has had to suffer through quite a bit of speculation of the sort found on these pages. I've heard a lot of people ask, "What the hell is a guy with all that money doing on the tour, taking money out of the pockets of guys who really need it?" They see him out on a golf course, sometimes struggling hard to finish fourteenth instead of fifteenth, and they wonder what's up, what's eating him that he should fight for a few extra bucks when he has a million of them at home. I'll tell you what's up. Frank is simply trying very hard to play the game he loves just as well as he can. Fourteenth place is better than fifteenth place, and so Frank is going to try and finish fourteenth.

I'll never forget a lesson in dedication I learned from him early one January morning after the 1958 Los Angeles Open. Frank had won the tournament at Los Angeles and I had finished just barely in the money. The tournament had ended on a Monday, and I had driven all night to get up to Pebble Beach near San Francisco, because I had to play a pre-qualifying round to get into the Crosby that year. I was staying with a family that had a house right by the seventeenth tee at Pebble Beach. I got there in time to grab a couple of hours' sleep, and very early in the morning I got up and went outside. I thought I'd head over to the third green, which is just behind the seventeenth tee, and hit some shots out of the sand trap. It was 7 o'clock and so early that I knew no one would be on the course. I was wrong. Frank Stranahan was on the course. Here it was only fifteen hours after the most important victory he had scored since becoming a professional. It was 7 A.M. and already he had played the first three holes and was standing on the seventeenth tee belting balls at the seventeenth green. That convinced me forever that Stranahan had as much right as anyone to be playing professional golf.

While Stranahan's decision to turn pro may have seemed odd to a lot of people, at least it was justified to a certain extent by his performance as an amateur. He had proved he could win. Only the overpowering lure of the tour can explain why so many others, less equipped to win, are out here. Take Billy Booe, for example. He spent a number of years on the tour, and I cite him not because he is exceptional or special, but just because his case is so typical.

Booe is a friendly, stocky guy from Bridgeport, Connecticut. He is also an Ivy Leaguer who played football for Yale and got a little bit of fame there because he converted 44 point-after-touchdown tries in a row during the late '40's. He was also a pretty good golfer, and in 1955 made it all the way to the semifinals of the National Amateur, the year it was held in Richmond, Virginia. He had meanwhile gotten married, had a child and worked his way up into a good spot with a Bridgeport foundation garment firm. He must have also been shooting plenty of rounds in the 60's at his golf club, because one day he did something that must have thoroughly perplexed his family and friends around Bridgeport. He threw up his job as if it were nothing more than a newspaper route, hopped in his car and rushed South to join the pro tour. I first met Billy when I played on the Caribbean tour in the winter of 1961. He had already been a touring pro for two or three years, but had barely made enough money to pay his caddy fees. "I just couldn't get golf out of my system," was how he explained his abrupt decision to turn pro. "I had to play a lot more than I had been playing and to see if I could make it on the tour against the best."

Billy also has a pretty good sense of humor about his abilities as a tournament player. After two rounds of the 1961 Caracas Open he had shot 70–68 and was in second place. It wasn't often he found himself in such a good position.

"When the boys back in the States read the paper and see

that Billy Booe is in second place in a tournament," he commented, "every rabbit on the tour is going to come rushing down to the Caribbean figuring there must be a lot of easy money to be had around here."

In spite of his lack of success as a tournament golfer, Booe is making a success out of his decision to turn pro. He now runs a golf club in Easton, Pennsylvania, and has become tournament supervisor of the Caribbean tour. I guess most people would rather be in the Caribbean for five weeks during the winter than in Bridgeport, Connecticut.

A more extreme example than Booe is supplied by a fellow I will call Jack Belsey. This guy had left a wife and children back home in Florida and had become the joke of the tour in the years shortly after I joined it. Belsey had never seen a paycheck that he had won on his own. The closest he came was a pro-amateur team event he won in Las Vegas. of not helping his team of amateurs on a single hole. Yet I have never seen a man more dedicated to golf than Belsey. He would spend hour upon hour out at the practice tee hoping that next week would be his week. It would be a different week and a different golf course. Maybe he would just start to get it going at last. Well, Belsey never did get it going. Jack made the 36-hole cut in only about one tournament, and I'll bet he played in almost a hundred. Everyone had to feel sorry for him. We'd chauffeur him from place to place, pick up his dinner checks every now and then, but there wasn't anything we could do about his golf game.
He came out of it with the unique and wonderful distinction
There are a lot of Belseys on the tour. A guy comes home one day and tells his wife, "I'm going to give this tour a try." So the wife remains behind, scrimping and saving to support herself and maybe a few kids. The Belsey types are

out on the tour not making a dime but trying to live it up just like prosperous players. They seldom see their family, they cat around, and eventually have a divorce suit on their hands. This type then starts to figure that he might have made it on the tour if only he hadn't been bogged down with a family and responsibilities. Eventually he finds out that the only responsibility he had really been bogged down with was trying to exploit a talent that was never there in the first place. When you start to think about these players, and there are more than there should be out here, the tour can seem like a sad and tragic caravan, not a golden one.

Fellows like Gerry Priddy, the former New York Yankee and Kansas City Athletics infielder, or John Brodie, the San Francisco Forty Niners star quarterback, have come out on the tour, but they would hardly fit into the Jack Belsey category. Priddy was thirty-nine when he turned pro, but he did so more as a lark than anything else. It was a pretty profitable lark, too, I understand. The word was that he was getting something like $20,000 a year to do public relations for Robert McCulloch, the big power-machinery manufacturer who has a place in Palm Springs reputed to have cost him $1,000,000. Priddy had been sporting some very good golf — 64's and 65's on courses he played a lot — and he suddenly got the itch to see how he could make out on the tour. McCulloch backed him and out he came for the winter season of 1960.

Everybody liked Gerry Priddy from the very beginning. He had a lot of guts, a former major league baseball star trying to see at thirty-nine how he could make out in another sport. He wasn't out here to forge his living, but he was testing himself, trying to meet a challenge. He was very pleasant to the younger players and pretty soon Gerry became a sentimental favorite. He was capable of playing good golf and we were all rooting for him to have a good tournament and finish in the money.

It finally happened. It wasn't often that Gerry even made the halfway cutdown, but at the 1960 Western Open in Detroit he started with a 71 and a 72 and was actually within striking distance of the lead. He finished with two good rounds, two 71's, finally finished in a tie for twentieth place and picked up a check for $230. The money itself didn't matter, it was what the money represented, a solidly played golf tournament. Everyone was so tickled that we went around slapping him on the back and saying "Now that Gerry's on the stick there won't be much left for the rest of us. Let's ship him back down to Kansas City."

I roomed with John Brodie for a while when he came out on the tour in 1959. We got along fine, even though he did complain that all my incoming telephone calls kept him awake at night. I was glad to have him there. He was married and could keep me out of trouble. John had been a good amateur and the people he used to play with must have gotten the idea he was quite a hotshot. So they talked him into turning pro and coming out on the tour. I don't think it was too hard to talk him into it, not because he thought he had the best golf game in the world, but because he was a terrific competitor. Anyone who has seen him play football for the Forty Niners knows that. Here was relentless competition for the off season.

The first few weeks Brodie was out with us a lot of the guys kind of fished him along during practice rounds and took some of his Forty Niner paycheck away from him. But it wasn't long before he had started to win it back from them. A great money player. At least in practice. I was always able to beat him, however. I'm not trying to knock John's ability as an athlete, God knows he's quite a bit better at football than I am, but I could beat him on the golf course. He was always trying to get to me, though. I recall one afternoon we were driving back to the motel in San Antonio after a practice round for the 1960 Texas Open. His wife had joined him on the tour for a couple of weeks and she was in the car with us.

"You know," John said, trying to convince me, "I think I can beat you."

"That's the difference between you and me, John," I said as graciously as possible, returning the needle, and also defining quite clearly why John was never going to make much of a success of pro golf, "you *think* you can beat me, but I *know* I can beat you."

Besides athletes, we sometimes take in stars from other professions. Like singer Don Cherry. A number of years ago Don had a couple of hit records, but I guess the best one he ever recorded was the Mr. Clean commercial. ("Mr. Clean gets rid of dirt and grime and grease in just a minute,/Mr. Clean will clean your whole house and everything that's in it.") He was making between $15,000 and $20,000 a year in residuals from that one. For years Cherry has traveled around the country wherever the tour was, singing in the local night-clubs and picking up silver trays in the amateur division of the tournament. I guess Don got sick of picking up trays when he could have been making some spendable silver, so in 1963 he turned pro. He had the credentials. Three times in his amateur days he was named to the Walker Cupteam, and once, in 1960, he had a chance to win the Open. If he had parred the last five holes he would have tied for first with Arnold Palmer, but he took a little gas, I guess, and actually finished four shots back. So Don has shown himself to be capable of picking up a good check from time to time. It hasn't hurt his singing career either. He still follows the tour, singing in local nightclubs and doing very well. He has become a great hit with the pros. We think he has a good voice and puts it over well. No one on the tour can understand why he hasn't become a bigger hit. Maybe, as with pro football, golf doesn't mix with singing too well.

More than professional athletes and singers have found it hard to resist the life, the competition and the money of the pro tour. So have professional men from a wide variety of fields. Dan Sikes, who was the twenty-second leading prize money earner in 1963 and won the important Doral Open, has passed his Florida bar exams. Julius Boros was a public accountant, a worthwhile profession, believe me, to bring with you on the tour. Al Balding drove a beer truck in Montreal, Ken Venturi sold cars, Cary Middlecoff was a dentist, Bo Winniger majored in psychology at Oklahoma A & M and then became a public relations man. There are a lot of people out on the tour who were born to play golf, to be sure, but there are also an awful lot of players who just came out, leaving other professions, because they couldn't stay away any longer.

The Stranahans, the Booes, the Priddys and the Brodies are just a small part of the group that travels from week to week around the country. In fact, the competition is getting so tough out here that it has become harder and harder for that type of player to have a chance. Palmer, Nicklaus and players of nearly that quality are the well-known names of pro golf, but there are another thirty players on the tour who have also proved themselves capable of winning tournaments, no matter how strong the field. A great many of them, like Palmer, were taught the game by a father who was a golf professional. Also, as I pointed out earlier, college golf has really blossomed as the training ground for the pro tour. These players knew when they joined the tour what it has taken me five years on the tour to learn: how to maintain consistency, to play the difficult shots that suddenly bob up at critical moments, to keep emotional control under pressure.

When I look back on the roller coaster career I began with about as much know-how as a housewife struggling to fix the television set, I wonder how I had the nerve to start out on the tour or stay with it as long as I did. Most of the players on the tour today at least got in on the ground floor. I climbed in through a basement window.

# 3 / *Too green for the gold*

DESPITE coming into golf from the bottom, I was spared the terrors and humiliations of life on the Ghost Squadron. I caddied a lot as a kid, took two country club jobs when I got older, played in several minor tournaments and a couple of major ones. I had a chance to take a pretty good look at the tour and at first didn't like what I saw. It seemed like a pretty big ocean. But finally, I screwed up my courage and made the decision to jump in. I was lucky that the breaking-in period was not too painful, because in a way I am a throwback to the old school. As I keep explaining (so you won't just think I was hopelessly slow as a student of professional golf), I had to learn on the tour most of the things that my touring comrades learned in college competition or tootling around the amateur circuit. But I had learned a bit, nibbled a bit, and was pretty enthusiastic when I finally joined up with the rest of the golfing nomads.

Only a few hours before I made the abrupt decision to go into golf as a profession, a career of that sort was as far from my mind as returning to the rocky hills of South Korea, where I had recently spent eleven months finishing out my two-year stint in the Marine Corps. Here it was October 1955, and I had just received my discharge and was driving home to Oakland from Camp Pendleton. The day was clear and balmy, about par for the course at that time of year in California, the motor of my secondhand Chevrolet was purring smoothly, and my spirits were floating along on the rhythmic music that poured from the car's radio. What lay ahead now that I was going back into civilian life? I didn't have much of an idea except that I could always get a job in one of the food canneries in the Bay area. That was something I had done plenty of during my high school days; during the summer, after school, at night. My father had died when I was three years old, leaving no insurance and three boys and a girl for my mother to raise in the industrial section of Oakland. Everyone in the family had to work pretty hard through the years to help make ends meet, and though I did everything I could to carry my share of the breadwinning burden I also did a little bit of hell-raising on the side.

I was pretty tough to handle in high school, ran with a rough crowd, and though we got into trouble quite a bit we were lucky enough to stay out of the local lockup. Those are years I would love to have the chance to do over. We got into trouble because we would sit around and booze it up from time to time, then start talking big and pump ourselves full of a lot of false courage. Phew! Talk about close calls! Thank goodness for golf. I began to caddy when I was twelve at the nearby Lake Chabot municipal golf course because I could pick up a couple of bucks a day that way. Then I began to play. How I loved to play! When I hit a good shot I got a strong thrill out of watching the ball hanging in the air and then the slow way it floated down to earth. The excitement of sinking a long putt was almost physical. I loved to play basketball, but that was a team sport, and the most important kick I got out of golf was the individual challenge. I didn't have to rely on anyone else. There was no team to blame for losing or to blame me for losing. A bad score was entirely my fault and a good one was entirely to my credit. Everything was right there in front of me and I could see it happening and know why it happened. By the time I was in my teens I loved the game so much that I would play hooky from school to be able to play golf. In the summers I would work the night shift at the cannery so that I could play golf during the day. The thought of making golf my life's work, however, had never occurred to me.

After finishing high school I had joined the Marines because I was at loose ends and couldn't think of anything better to do. I served in Korea as an observer with the artillery corps, but the fighting was over by that time and I never got into any trouble there. When I got back to the States, I joined the camp golf team (also because I was at loose ends and couldn't think of anything better to do), and played unspectacularly in the All-Marine Championship at Parris Island, all the way across the country, and in the All-Service Championship at Langley Air Force Base in Virginia. Now here I was on the high road back home. My Marine Corps hitch was over and I had to face the world again.

As I sailed through Hayward, just east of San Francisco, a police siren cut through the music of the car radio. I pulled over to the side of the highway and a police car from the county sheriff's office pulled over in front of me. I thought that this was a hell of a way to get back into civilian life, but the man who climbed out of the car turned out to be an old golfing companion, Jerry Kroeckel of Oakland. We never did get around to discussing the fact that I had been going seventy in a fifty-five-mile zone.

Jerry and I had played a lot of golf together before I went into the Marines and we had both won the Oakland City Amateur Championship. We lit up cigarettes and talked a little bit there by the side of the road. When he heard that my plans for the future seemed to reach no further than working a stamping machine at the Gerber Food cannery in Oakland, he told me that the San Francisco Golf Club was interviewing applicants for a spot as an assistant on its professional staff and that I should try to get the job. I went right over.

There were twelve applicants for the position, but the head professional at the club, John Geersten, seemed to like the cut of my jib and I was lucky enough to get hired. I was now a golf professional. The job wasn't much. I worked around the golf shop selling equipment and clothing, cleaned the members' clubs and swept floors. I was paid about what I was worth, $225 a month. But if the job wasn't much to talk about, the club itself was. The San Francisco Golf Club is one of the poshest in the Bay area. Its membership is drawn from the high command of some of San Francisco's most successful businesses, from the area's most prominent and wealthy families. Working there proved to be quite an experience. I learned how to dress (conservatively), how to behave in polite society (relaxed, but attentive good manners), and how to play golf with a professional flair (well enough, in fact, to qualify for the 1956 U.S. Open in Rochester, New York).

The 1956 U.S. Open was my first taste of big-time tournament golf and big-time tournament players. This is roughly equivalent to a rookie's breaking into major league baseball at the World Series. I was so ignorant and so green that you could hardly distinguish me from the grass of the fairways. The experience was so overpowering that it almost kept me out of tournament golf forever, but at least I did begin to learn that playing competitive golf involved something more than throwing your golf ball down on the first tee and hitting it until you had finished 18 holes. For the first time I learned about the cut — the reduction I mentioned earlier that takes place halfway through every tournament, cutting the field down to a more workable size. At the Open after 36 holes the field is reduced to the lowest fifty scorers, or anyone tied for fiftieth place. The hundred players who fail to survive the cut go home and the rest play the final 36 holes on Saturday, carrying their scores forward so that the final total will be based on 72 holes of play. On the PGA tour it is customary to cut the field to the sixty lowest scores after 36 holes. These players then finish out the tournament with 18 holes on Saturday and another 18 on Sunday.

For the first time I learned how to register at the club, how to find my locker, how to get my caddy, how to obtain coupon books that entitled me to eat at the club for half price, and in general how to comport myself around the site of a tournament I was playing in. I got all my information kind of left-handed, from clean-up boys and spectators — but I got it. By the time I played in my next tournament (the Western Open in San Francisco some four months later), my green complexion was at least a little paler.

For the first time I also met the big names of professional golf. Or rather, I didn't meet them; stood around and stared at them goggled-eyed would be more accurate. Prior to the Open these players were simply important names that I had read about in books, magazines and newspapers. I had never even seen any of them play. I got a big charge from seeing Mike Souchak getting a haircut in the club barbershop. I actually sat at a big long table in the club grillroom and ate lunch with the likes of Sam Snead and Ben Hogan, with Cary Middlecoff, who had won the Open in 1949 and was to win it again that year, with Doug Ford, the 1955 PGA champion, with Jack Burke, the recent Masters champion. I kept my eyes and ears open and was very impressed. These players impressed me so much, in fact, that I crept over the hill to Oak Hill's adjoining 18-hole course and did my practicing there.

To understand how I got to the Open in the first place is to understand why I felt so out of place there. I had become a fairly good golfer at that time, but as jobs went, mine at the San Francisco Golf Club was nothing more than that of a glorified golfing busboy. In late May 1956 the sectional qualifying rounds for the U.S Open for our area were being held in San Francisco at the California Country Club. Eddie Lowery, a Lincoln-Mercury dealer who was at that time a big man on the United States Golf Association board of directors, went around encouraging a lot of the young assistant professionals to sign up and try to qualify. His purpose, no doubt, was to swell the size of the local qualifying field, and therefore earn for the area more qualifying spots. This way more of San Francisco's good golfers would have a chance to make the trip and play in the Open. I doubt if he imagined that anyone of my untried abilities would be able to play well enough to qualify.

Surprisingly enough, I did. Along with about six or seven others. It was a tribute to my valuable position at the club and the big name I had made for myself there that when the local newspapers carried the names of the qualifiers and identified me as working at the San Francisco Golf Club, a dozen or so members called the sports editors in town to inform them that they had made a mistake, that no one by the name of Tony Lema worked at their club. It is also a tribute to the generosity of the membership that when the misunderstanding was eventually straightened out, they raised $600 to pay my expenses for the long trip to Rochester.

It was my first trip to the Northeast and I was awed, especially by the magnificent tree-shaded golf course, by far the finest I had ever seen. Despite all this, I played pretty well. I was paired for the first two rounds with a nervous young amateur who sprayed his shots all over the place, but at least we had no gallery to bother us. The first day we played so early we walked along the fairways through a spray of dew. The next day we were sent out so late you'd almost think we had been hired to clean up papers and bring in the flagsticks as we went along. On the last hole of the second day I hit a terrific 5-iron shot to three feet from the hole, and the course was so deserted at that late hour that there wasn't even anybody there to applaud. The birdie I made, however, gave me a total of 148 (a 77 and a 71) for 36 holes and I went back to my downtown hotel feeling rather pleased with myself. After supper I was in the lobby reading a newspaper when I heard some people, obviously spectators, talking about what score would qualify for the last two rounds.

"What's this?" I asked one of them. "Doesn't everyone play tomorrow?"

"No," was the answer. "There's a cutoff and 149 will probably make it."

My score of 148 was therefore probably good enough to keep me in the tournament, but as I staggered up to bed I couldn't help thinking how embarrassing it would have been if I had bogeyed the last hole for a 150, instead of birdying it for a 148, and then had shown up at the club the next day expecting to play two more rounds.

I played two more rounds the next day, but I might as well not have. There was a mob of about ten thousand people around the first tee, waiting for the leaders like Peter Thomson, Middlecoff, Ted Kroll, Julius Boros, Hogan, etc., to go off, and I was so nervous I almost missed my drive completely. I finished up with a 79 and an 81 for a tournament total of 308, a score that beat an amateur named John Garrett by a stroke, and no one else. But at least I'd made the cut and picked up a check for $200. The experience of playing the Open, however, came a little too fast, and the whole thing made about as much impression on me as surf does breaking over a rock. I had picked up a little tournament savoir-faire, to be sure, but I was more determined than ever that tournament savoir-faire, since I would never be a tournament golfer, was something I could do without.

A few months later, in October, this resolve was hardened. The Western Open was played that year at the Presidio golf course in San Francisco. Since it was being held nearby, I decided to play in it. The first day I was scheduled to tee off so late that I was able to do a full day's work at the club before I went over to the tournament. The next day I teed off so early in the morning that my pants were wet with dew right up to the knees when I finished. It was 9:30 in the morning and people were just coming in for breakfast when I left the club and returned to a full day's work in my golf shop.

My first three rounds were a 76, a 71, and a 72. This gave me a 54-hole total of 219, and since similar scores are paired together on the PGA tour after the first two rounds, I was placed in a threesome with Dow Finsterwald and Bob Rosburg. Bob was a local boy whom I had heard about but had never seen before. He was already a big shot on the pro tour, having won several tournaments, including the San Diego Open just the week before. Dow was pretty big, too, having won a few tournaments himself. There I was, nothing but a shop assistant paired with two of the top players in the game. Finsterwald put on an exhibition of golf the like of which I had never seen. He drove the ball perfectly and practically hit the hole with every iron shot he hit into the greens. Here was where I really got the idea that I did not want to make touring golf my livelihood. He shot a 66 on the par 72 Presidio course and I said to myself, "If this is the way I have to play golf before I can make it on the tour, then the tour is no place for me." Finsterwald's virtually flawless round of golf gave him a 66 and put him into fifth place. My final total of 291 for 72 holes placed me in a tie for twenty-second and earned me $185. The U.S. Open and the Western Open had given me my first taste of tour tournaments with the big-timers. I felt very inferior. I just wanted to pick up my meager little check, go back to the San Francisco Golf Club and happily clean the clubs that the members would use that day.

In another way, however, the experience had been valuable. The first time you do anything it is difficult, but now at least I knew how to pick my way through the confusion that surrounds a big tournament, how to go about checking in at a course, where and what the practice areas were. How to find my way around. But as far as I was concerned, the tour seemed about as far off as the foreign legion. I was simply not good enough and never would be good enough to play on it. It took a rather astonishing tournament, played only three months later in the tiny little desert town of El Centro, near the California-Mexico border, to begin to convince me otherwise.

# 4 / *Strange places and split purses*

E L Centro is a small cabbage and lettuce growing community tucked into the Imperial Valley in Southern California. Its residents are for the most part tough, hard-working general produce farmers who have prospered through diligence. They play cards for pretty high stakes and they even have a pleasant little golf course, the Barbara Worth Country Club. I had come to El Centro in late January 1957 as part of a tournament golf vacation. In a few weeks I would be starting as head professional at a nine-hole municipal course in the gambling and lake resort of Elko, Nevada. Eddie Lowery had lent me $500 toward my expenses at three or four tournaments that I wanted to play in between leaving my job at San Francisco and starting at Elko. I was able to pay him back very quickly. The first week I had played in the Bing Crosby pro-am, and had not done too well. The next week I had played at the Caliente Open in Tijuana and had not even made the cut.

Tijuana is one of the great honky-tonk towns of the West — gambling, loose women, crowded, narrow and dirty streets, tiny little shops that sell all kinds of junk to tourists from across the California border, and a race track. It is therefore an interesting place to hold a golf tournament. There, at least, I had my first fairly close contact with one of the tour's major performers. On Saturday morning I was out on the practice tee trying to get in a little work before I headed for El Centro.

I was complaining very loudly about not making the cut at Caliente, and when Jay Hebert heard my ringing voice he strolled over to take a look at me.

"That's a shame," he said. "How did you do last week in the Crosby?"

Now I was talking to the man who had won the Crosby, his first victory in seven years on the tour, and I managed to stammer out that I had qualified for the last round and barely picked up a check.

Then Jay asked me how long I had been out on the tour, and when I told him how limited my experience was he was quite surprised. He said missing the cut was something that happened frequently to even the most experienced and talented players and I shouldn't let it discourage me in the slightest. This chat with Jay was not only good for my morale, but it also convinced me that these guys out on the tour were actually human and not just high-powered golfing machines.

Now I had come over for the Imperial Valley Open as the final stop on my vacation trip. The elite of the pro tour were playing that week in the Thunderbird Invitational at Palm Springs, and the Imperial Valley Open was a minor tournament, with a total prize money of only $5000, that had been put on for the scrubs, the has-beens and may-bes of the tour. There are many such byways on the golf circuit. Lionel Hebert, the chubby member of the Hebert brother golfing twosome, who won the PGA Championship later that year, was on hand. So was Al Balding, the tall former truck driver from Canada who had already won a tour tournament and would win three more in 1957. Long-hitting Paul Harney, who had come out on the tour right out of Holy Cross College, was also in the field. He went on to win two big tournaments in 1957. Tough little Smiley Quick, who had won the National Public Links Championship before turning pro, was there, and so was Fred Wampler, who had won at Los Angeles in 1954. For a minor tournament, the field was a pretty strong one.

I had stayed over in Tijuana an extra couple of days to practice and didn't arrive at the Barbara Worth course until late Monday afternoon, in time for a nine-hole practice round. That was all I was able to play before the tournament started. A two-day combination professional-amateur tournament was put on Tuesday and Wednesday, and the course was closed to those of us with too little status to be invited to play in it. For two days, instead of being able to learn something about the layout, we were obliged to sit on our hands, or at the club bar, and we were furious. I was so mad I felt suicidal. On one of the nights I went downtown in a tee shirt and levis, found a dingy little joint in a side alley where a game of low-ball was in progress, and I sat in.

With the aid of a few drinks, some headstrong betting and some exceptionally good cards I was able to stay ahead, and finally after a couple of hours I had a chance to win a really big pot. The house rules specified that a perfect low was an ace-two-three-four-five, and that was exactly what I held. The group of guys I was playing with looked mean enough to slit my throat for two bits, but another player in the game held what he thought was a pretty good hand — an ace-two-three-four-six. He kept betting the pot up and up until it reached well over $100. I kept betting and he kept raising and pretty soon I began to get a little scared. I knew I had him beat, but I figured that if I cleaned him too badly he might decide to do something nasty. Finally, I called. When I showed my unbeatable hand everyone looked pretty sullen. I quickly decided I'd had enough cards for one night, because

I didn't want it to be my last. I grabbed up all the bills in the pot and walked out the door into the alley with the paper still in my hand. If anyone jumped me with a knife I was just going to hand the cash over and say, "It's yours. With my compliments." I figured my life was worth more than $150, but I guess I moved so fast no one had a chance to challenge me. I sprinted to the car and was back in my hotel even before my knees had started to shake.

I spent most of my low-ball winnings at the clubhouse bar during the week — I had spells in those days when I could really lush it up — and played some pretty mediocre golf for the first two rounds. On the third day, however, I shot a good 67 and went into the final 18 holes, tied for fifth place, but still six shots back of leader Paul Harney. I didn't think I had much chance to win, but I was determined to fight for a nice sweet chunk of prize money.

The Barbara Worth golf course was dead flat and the first desert course I had ever seen. The grass on the fairways was as brown as straw, while the greens, which were watered thoroughly every night, were the bright glittering green that only desert grass, when it is given plenty of water, can display. The course was an old one and the trees that lined each fairway were very high. If you didn't hit the ball straight you needed a sharp ax to get it out of trouble.

During the first eight holes of the final round I was in and out of all the trees on the course. I had stayed even with par simply by sheer determination and the aid of some very long putts. Then on the ninth hole my game jelled. This was a short par four hole and I hit my tee shot right to the edge of the green and then chipped the ball into the cup for an eagle two. I birdied the tenth hole, sank long putts for pars on the eleventh and twelfth. By the time I was walking down the sixteenth fairway I was four strokes under par and hoping that I might earn a check of about $500 or $600. At that point I looked through the trees bordering the sixteenth and saw the two leaders — Harney and Bob Inman — using irons off the twelfth tee. The fairway on the twelfth hole was narrow and they were being cautious in an effort to keep the ball straight. I had used a full driver on that hole and thought, "That's pretty good. Here are those two cautiously dillydallying around. They might just outchoke each other over there and I might just slip in and win this tournament."

Actually, I didn't really think so. I finished by sinking a long putt for a birdie on the seventeenth hole, and a putt of at least 60 feet on the last hole for another birdie, but my extraordinary final round of 65 did not seem good enough to make up a six-stroke deficit. Harney could easily shoot 70 on this course and beat me by at least a shot.

I returned to my favorite place, the bar, and drank down three Scotch and waters. I was just reaching for the fourth drink when someone came running in and said that Harney would have to get his ball into the hole in two shots from the front of the eighteenth green just to tie me. I pushed the drink away and floundered outside in time to see Harney chip his ball up and then drop in a seven-foot putt.

The two of us were summoned to the first tee by a tournament official for a sudden death play-off. To say that I was slightly peeved at myself for belting down a few quick ones when I might have anticipated this situation would be quite an understatement, but maybe the drinks took my mind off the pressure. At this particular tournament first place paid $1000 and second place $700. As we prepared to hit off an official suggested that we split the difference in prize money, a common practice in play-offs, and play only for the honor of winning the tournament. Harney had been on the tour for a couple of years and had made some high finishes in important tournaments, but I just wasn't about to split anything with anybody. This official was furious when I said, even before Harney had a chance to express himself on the subject, that I would have nothing to do with such an arrangement. "Who the hell do you think you are, anyway?" the official asked. "I'm the guy in this blasted play-off," I told him.

It was my honor and I hit a pretty good drive on the hole, a short par four, but Harney ripped one about 40 yards past my drive and was pin high to the right of the green. I hit the middle of the green with a wedge shot, but it didn't stop quickly enough and rolled to the back edge about 15 or 20 feet above the hole. Harney chipped his ball about four feet below the hole. I then hit a putt that rolled down the green and straight into the cup for a birdie three. It was about the tenth long putt that I had stroked into the cup that day and this apparently jarred Paul so much that he barely stumbled in his four-footer.

The next hole was another short par four, but the fairway curved to the right around a clump of trees and a pond guarded the left side of the green. The best way to play the hole was to drive the ball into the left side of the fairway and be able to hit an approach shot from that relatively safe angle. This was too simple for me, so I whipped my tee shot way over to the right and into the trees. Fortunately it hit a tree and kicked out to the edge of the fairway. Paul then hit a beautiful long drive, down the left side of the fairway in perfect position for his next shot. If I hadn't still been feeling the effects of my visit at the bar I would have known that this was the end for me. I was partially stymied by a tree and would have to hit a fantastic shot to get the ball on the green.

I finally decided to use a 7-iron and aim the ball right at the pond to the left and try to hit the shot in such a way that it would fade into the green along a left to right trajectory. I hit the ball firmly and it flew toward the pond. Then, just as it seemed that the ball was heading toward a watery end, it reacted to the spin I had given it and faded right in about 10 or 12 feet from the hole. Harney must have figured by this time that he was contending with a freak who used black magic. His 9-iron shot left him 25 feet short of the hole and his first putt was still short. I then got over my ball and using still more of that black magic putted it straight into the hole to win the play-off and the tournament.

At that moment I was not thinking about the wisdom I had shown in rejecting the tournament official's request that Harney and I divide first and second place prize money equally, but I have had reason to think about it since. Actually, there was never any harm in the practice, because not once did it ever change the result of a single stroke or a single golf tournament. Golf is a risky business and it was just another method that players once used to minimize the risks. The man was merely attempting to invoke a practice the players themselves had initiated. The arrangement has met with a great deal of criticism from people outside the pro tour, however, and so the PGA tournament bureau has officially banned players from entering into any such agreements.

In the old days of the professional circuit, just before and just after World War II, there was not much prize money to compete for and only about ten players could actually make a living at it. It was a common practice for two or three players to form a little syndicate. They would agree to share and share alike all prize money that syndicate members won. The team usually broke up when one of the players found himself playing so well that he carried the rest of the group on his own earnings, but at least it was a way for newcomers to the tour to find out who could make it and who could not.

Another method of purse splitting involved making a deal just prior to a very rich tournament or one that offered a special fat prize for a hole-in-one. In the middle 1950's George S. Mays, who owned a highly successful management consulting firm, used to put on a real three-ring circus of a golf tournament that paid a first prize of $50,000. In 1957, the year he won the U.S. Open, Dick Mayer made a deal with Al Besselink prior to this tournament. If either of them won the tournament the other would get 10 percent of the winner's purse. Mayer won the tournament and Bessie, who finished tied for twenty-first, 10 shots back of Mayer, picked up a $5000 slice of the winner's pie. I gather from some of the other players who shared their purses with Besselink at other events that the tall, curly-haired blond had consistently good luck in picking his partners for a split of the purse.

Something similar happened in 1959, the year pudgy Joe Campbell shot a hole-in-one at the Palm Springs Desert Classic that was worth $50,000. The happiest man on the course when Joe scored his ace, however, was a good-looking, thoroughly unknown player named Buddy Sullivan. A pre-tournament deal gave Buddy a $25,000 share of Campbell's prize. This was twice as much as Campbell got out of it. Joe was being supported on the tour at the time by a prosperous sports fan back in Nashville, Tennessee. He paid all of Joe's expenses on the tour and in return got half of all Joe's winnings. So Joe's share was only $12,500.

At the 1958 Greensboro Open I was in a good position to win the tournament after 36 holes. A torrential rainstorm had postponed one round, so the final two rounds were going to be played on the same day, a Sunday. Al Balding was leading the tournament with a 136, but I was in second place only two shots back. I was in my motel room watching television when a fellow pro, a onetime insurance salesman from Minnesota, came by and suggested that we split fifty-fifty the prize money we earned the following day. I had this guy by two or three shots and didn't much care for his way of doing business anyway, so I turned him down. Apparently this player had tried to make the same deal with several others, figuring that he wasn't good enough to win the tournament himself but might by this method get a share of the $2000 first prize. He eventually won a check for $500 or $600 less than I did.

The question of purse splitting came to a head late in the 1962 season. In September, Jack Nicklaus, Arnold Palmer and Gary Player had competed in a televised exhibition called the World Series of Golf. First prize was $50,000, second was $15,000 and third was $10,000. There was a great deal of speculation during that weekend, by fans, the press, and the rest of the players on the tour, that these three might have agreed to split the total purse into three $25,000 shares. The three were pretty good friends and even had the same business agent. The situation was such that it excited the suspicions of a lot of people. In this case no real tournament title was involved. The only justification for playing, therefore, was in the first prize involved. The gallery at the course was limited to eight thousand and the sole purpose of the exhibition was to put on a television show. If the three players had secretly divided the money evenly, the millions watching the show on TV to see who would win the enormous first prize would be defrauded. Palmer, Player and Nicklaus are much too honest to have split on this occasion, but speculation about splitting the purse at the World Series of Golf led to speculation that it went on at other times, which, in fact, it did.

"We certainly did not split at the World Series," Gary Player said, "but I'm not ashamed to admit that I've done it at other times. When the play-off is a sudden death one that may not go more than one hole, it isn't fair to have all that money, money that you are really entitled to share because you have tied for first, riding on a couple of shots."

Palmer admitted that he indulged in this practice too. "I'll go either way," he said. "If a guy wants to split, okay. If he doesn't, that's okay too. I've always played for the title, which is very important. Even with a split there is never any lack of incentive. Everything depends on winning out here. The guy who finishes second, in a play-off or anything else, might as well have finished twentieth. Nobody remembers who finished second." In this case, Nicklaus was the winner.

The vital point in this whole matter is that though prize splitting has been a continuous practice on the tour for many years, never has the gallery or the television audience been deprived of a 100-percent effort by any player. It is a rare tournament title that isn't worth a great deal more than the immediate prize money it pays. I ought to know. I've turned down purse splitting offers because I just didn't think they were fair to anybody concerned, but in the five years it took me to win my first big tournament there were a dozen times when I would gladly have given away all of the winner's purse just for the opportunity to be the winner.

The 1957 Imperial Valley Open was not one of these important titles, but you can still imagine how elated I was as I walked back to the clubhouse with Harney, our caddies and about a thousand spectators. The pros and cons of purse splitting couldn't have bothered me less. All of a sudden I had won a tournament and a check for $1000, which looked like an awfully big paycheck to me. I didn't think that I had played particularly well, but at least I'd fooled people into thinking I could. When I heard my name coming over the radio and read it in the local newspapers, I had even begun to fool myself.

This was a vital little push, and it is the push that has tumbled many, many players — pro or amateur — out onto the tour. I wasn't completely conscious of it at the time, but it was then that I decided how I really wanted to make my living. That little tournament was also valuable in another respect. I had won it even though I had started so badly. I had kept working hard, even though I was not playing well, and when suddenly things began to break my way I was able to take advantage of the breaks. In the depression years of 1959 and '60, when I was throwing clubs, losing my temper and giving up at the first sign of bad luck, I forgot the lesson I should have learned at El Centro. It was when I finally began to reflect back on what had happened there, and what could happen again if I kept working to save every stroke I could, even when strokes didn't seem to be worth saving, that I began to play golf again the way it should be played.

With that check for $1000 in my wallet I would probably have gone right out on the tour then and there, but of course I was contracted to start work at Elko, Nevada, and I went up there instead. Thus began a summer in which I enriched my golfing experience, depleted my bank account, and formed an association with the strange, erratic man who finally made it possible for me to start out on the tour.

# 5 / *A rookie learns — or else*

THE place I had now chosen to settle down in for a year
was a tiny little desert town of about six thousand people
situated in the northeast corner of Nevada. It was strictly the
poor man's Las Vegas. It contained three casinos and a couple
of nightclubs and served as a resort chiefly for people from
Idaho and Utah. Only occasionally was it honored by a visit
from a free-spending West Coast vacationer. There is not
much to do in Elko except drink and gamble. Any visitor
with a little energy left over could play golf. While my job
as head professional at the nine-hole municipal golf course was
hardly a magnificent one, it did give me plenty of time to
practice and play.

My duties consisted of running the modest pro shop, setting
up tournaments for the men and women who played there,
and giving a few lessons. Needless to say the work was not
exactly arduous. My after-work routine was unvaried. A few
martinis with a friend before dinner — sometimes no dinner
at all, just martinis — and then over to one of the local gambling casinos for the rest of the evening. The gamblers in
Elko got all of my money and a few IOU's in addition. From
me the local bank never got a dime.

I also competed in a number of local golf tournaments. I
won the Idaho Open and the Montana Open, but every time
I played I was creating an imaginary little drama in my head.

"This isn't the Montana Open," I'd say to myself, "it's the Western Open. And I'm not playing with Walt Harris, or Dick Cramer or Cliff Whittle. These guys against me are Finsterwald, Rosburg and Middlecoff." And the year was never 1957. It was always the future: 1962 or '63 or '64 or '65 or '66. This activity sounds childish, but if you are the pro at a nine-hole course in a backwater of Nevada it's surprising the number of things you will do to put a bit of juice in the daily routine. Besides, I was getting pretty hopped up about going out on the tour. I'd often go out for a nine-hole practice round and play two balls — one mine, the other Ben Hogan's. Hogan never had a chance; nor did he on the practice putting green, where I'd usually putt with three balls. One was Hogan's, one was Snead's and one was mine. Sam's ball would slide by the hole just a little too far to the right, Hogan's would miss on the left, and then Tony Lema would bang his putt right into the middle of the hole for the winning birdie.

One of the people I saw quite a bit of around Elko was a pudgy young playboy from a large West Coast city. Since he will emerge from this narrative as something less than an All-American boy I will just call him Crocker. He popped in from Sun Valley frequently to drink, gamble and play a little golf. He indulged heavily in all three activities, but the only one at which he showed any particular proficiency was the first. Crocker proved to be a delightful companion and also took quite an interest in my golfing career. We drank, gambled and played golf together and one weekend flew over to Sun Valley, where Crocker owned a house, in a plane owned by Cliff Whittle, another pro from the area. Whittle, Crocker and I were scheduled to play in a pro-amateur tournament. We stayed with Crocker, and after the tournament the three of us went back to his house for drinks.

"Crock," Whittle said rather suddenly, "why don't you put Tony on the tour?" Crocker had soaked up quite a few high-balls by then, but he never even changed the expression on his face.

"Fine," he said. "I'll do it."

That is how I got on the tour. Change a few details here and there and you get a pretty typical picture of how a lot of golfers get started in tournament golf.

My new sponsor and I shook hands on an oral agreement that called for him to advance me $200 a week. I would pay that money back out of my prize winnings and would in addition give him one-third of anything I won over that. He also helped with the payments on a new car, a Plymouth, which I took out on the tour with me. The arrangement was a standard one among young players joining the tournament circuit for the first time and it seemed ideal. It worked so successfully the first year that we agreed to put it in writing after that. A mere formality. I assumed that he was my friend and he stated that through his interest in my career he would also teach me to be a good businessman. His prediction proved to be 100 percent correct, but because my first assumption proved to be so wrong the lesson became a costly one. Signing a contract with the man I thought at the time to be a wealthy sporting philanthropist proved to be one of the most interesting mistakes of my life.

But now thoughts of contracts and options on options were as far from my mind as the fruit canneries in Oakland. The idea of being out on the tour, with nothing to worry about except moving from tournament to tournament, seemed like something from the daydreams of childhood. I was soon to learn that playing the tour involved considerably more than playing golf, but I was just an elated young rookie who could hardly wait to tee it up in the big time.

As I said, the first big tournament of the year is always the Los Angeles Open. It is a rich tournament with a long and exciting history and a list of winners of which even the Masters or the Open would be proud: Lawson Little, Jimmy Demaret, Ben Hogan, Sam Snead, Lloyd Mangrum, Gene Littler, Doug Ford and Arnold Palmer, just to name a few. It is an important tournament to win and even a prestigious one at which to finish among the top ten. Every touring pro and any Californian with at least four clubs and a bag wants to play in it. The result is that after all the players exempt from pre-tournament qualifying have entered, there is a stampede of players trying to fill the few remaining spots. About 350 golfers must pre-qualify for the twenty or thirty openings available. One way to avoid the terrors and insecurity of pre-tournament qualifying is to make the 36-hole cut-off at the preceding tournament. This isn't exactly a piece of cake either, but many players make a special trip to play in the last event of each year with the hope that they will make the 36-hole cut-off — say in the top thirty or forty — and thus qualify to play at Los Angeles. At least that way they have two shots at it.

This was what I resolved to do. Unfortunately the last tournament on the 1957 schedule was the December 12–15 Mayfair Inn Open in Sanford, Florida, sponsored by the New York baseball Giants, who owned the inn. This was a long trip and would cost me something like $500, but if I finished thirtieth or better in Sanford I would be in business at Los Angeles, and it seemed worth the risk. As it turned out, I finished not only in the money, I finished high in the money. After a moderately slow start I shot 66–69–67 for the last three rounds and won $725 by finishing in a tie for sixth. Now I wasn't playing in the Idaho Open with Walt Harris, Dick Cramer or Cliff Whittle. My romantic imaginings of the summer had been transmitted to reality and the fact was almost as good as the dream.

After I had finished my third round at Sanford — I was through early in the day — I went out to follow some of the better players in case there were any secrets to championship golf that I didn't know about. I watched Bob Toski and Jay Hebert play some of the holes I had played earlier. I was surprised to find that they had no secret at all. Outside of the fact that they seemed to be knocking their approach shots consistently closer to the flagstick, they played each hole almost exactly as I had. They had consistency, I saw, but that was something I would pick up as I gained experience. The trick I had overlooked — and did not really learn for four years — was that something very vital and very important was going on in their heads. On the surface there was no indication that this consistency of theirs — and of every fine player — stems from an emotional and mental discipline that keeps him working hard over every shot no matter how badly he may want to give up, no matter how badly he may want to wrap his clubs around the handiest tree, no matter how heartily he may be cursing the ill luck that caused a bad bounce. These veteran players seemed, however, to be hitting the ball the same way I was. I said to myself, "What the hell, I can do the same thing. It's just a question of a little time."

It took me more than a little time. I was to survive a checkbook full of fines and a lot of temper tantrums before I realized that playing golf was 30 percent physical and 70 percent mental. Lose control of the mental side and you were only 30 percent a golfer. A player who wanted to win, therefore, had to be mentally tough enough to keep bearing down for every stroke of every hole of every round of every tournament. There are some days, of course, when even an IBM machine cannot concentrate. But these days have to be few and far between or the victories will be few and far between. Emotional stability under pressure is not something that comes easily to all of us. Some are lucky enough to be born with it. The rest simply must practice it until it becomes second nature. There is no other way to be a truly successful golfer.

I had not yet learned the important lesson that tournament golf was to teach. But by osmosis I was picking up pretty quickly some of the other tricks as I started out on the tour at Los Angeles, drove up the California coast to the Monterey Peninsula in my shiny new Plymouth for the Bing Crosby pro-am, came back down to Tijuana, then headed out into Arizona, across Texas and on into Louisiana and Florida as winter ended and spring arrived. A rookie's life on the tour can be a pretty lonely one. Young players come and go like migrant birds and few veteran players have the time or the patience to go out of their way to make things comfortable for a newcomer. Some veterans are hard on the rookie and some are not, but a cocky newcomer who asserts himself a little too aggressively is likely to wind up behind the 8-iron. The first day I arrived in Phoenix, for instance, I got to the course late on a Monday afternoon and had time for only a nine-hole practice round. Little Jerry Barber was about to go out and I thought it would be a treat to play a few holes with a player I had heard so much about. What I hadn't heard about was that Jerry Barber can be just about the tartest player on the tour when he decides to be. I summoned up some courage and asked him if I could play a few holes with him. He said yes, but from his tone of voice one might have thought I had asked him to wash out a pair of my socks.

At the first hole, a short par five on which the green could be reached with two long straight shots, I hit a poor second shot and quickly dropped another ball, since it was a practice round, to see if I had used the right club. Suddenly a piercing voice cut through my concentration.

"Hey, kid," Barber howled at me, "you can cut that out right now. Don't you know you're not allowed to hit practice shots here?"

Well, I hadn't known or I wouldn't have done it, and I jumped right out of my golf spikes I was so startled. There are a lot of little rules on the tour and they take a great deal of time to learn. Barber, with reason born of experience, probably thought I was a fresh young punk trying to get away with something. In this case I was not, but it might not have been that obvious. On the tour you have to learn things quickly, and Barber, though it made the hair on the back of my neck stand up like the bristles in a hairbrush, was teaching me the quickest way he knew.

Of course there is another way, too. Contrast my Phoenix experience with the one I had at the Buick Open in Flint, Michigan, that same year. It was the first time I had ever had anything to do with Arnold Palmer and I have been a firm admirer ever since. The traps at the Warwick Hills Country Club, where the Buick Open is held each year, are very difficult to play out of, because the sand in them is coarse and filled with tiny pebbles. I was having a great deal of trouble with them during my practice rounds, so late one afternoon I went out to the third green with my caddy and about ten golf balls to practice these difficult explosion shots. Technically, it was a violation of a tournament rule stating that players shouldn't practice on the course. I was out there blasting to the green when suddenly Palmer and Dow Finsterwald appeared over a hill, playing a few practice holes before calling it a day. Palmer spotted me and came over.

"I know that you know you're not supposed to be practicing this way," he said, but in a calm, pleasant manner. "I guess you need the practice and you probably feel you need it very badly. But so do all of us. What you're doing will mark up the green and make it difficult for the greenskeeper to keep it in shape. I'm not a policeman or anything, and I'm not going to order you to stop, but I can suggest a way of practicing that will be just as good for you and not nearly as hard on the golf course. Play a few holes and deliberately hit a shot now and then into one of these sand traps."

Finsterwald nodded agreement and the two of them then played on through. Palmer had won the Masters two months previously and was just about the biggest shot on the tour. I had won nothing except a few checks and was about as big-time as a beebee. Yet Palmer had handled the situation with such grace that in no way did I feel humiliated. Instead, I felt great.

There were numerous other lessons to be learned the first time around the pro circuit; not just rules but rules of living. At the Los Angeles Open, for instance, I checked into my hotel after driving down from Oakland, then discovered that it was a ninety-minute drive from the golf course. I also learned that once a rookie got to the golf course no one particularly cared whether he was there or not. The registration desk never could seem to get my name right and the locker room attendant always seemed much too busy to assign me a locker. When he did I was usually asked to share my locker with another player who possessed a similar lack of status.

It didn't take me long, either, to learn that there is quite a bit of class distinction on the pro tour. This distinction is both written and unwritten. The fairest and most obvious one is in the way the tournament pairings are worked out. When I first came out, the newcomers were always sent out early in the morning or late in the afternoon. The established stars got the choice starting times. Lesser lights became known as "dew sweepers" because the course was always dripping wet when they teed off, or the Litter Brigade because they went off so late in the day that they played through a sea of ice cream wrappers, beer cups and pop bottles.

This inequality in starting times has been pretty much eliminated by the PGA tournament committee in recent years, but a caste system of pairing the players in the first two rounds still exists. In this case, however, it is a good caste system with a purpose. To decide who will play with whom for the first two rounds Doc Giffin, or whoever is working as the PGA publicity man traveling with the tour, first separates the starting field into four categories. Group one consists of all previous tournament winners; in group two are the non-winners who have been picking up big checks from week to week; group three consists of the players who have not been picking up big checks but who have been at least getting into the money pretty consistently; group four consists of everybody else — the local pros, the local amateurs, and the members of the Ghost Squadron lucky enough to have qualified for that week's tournament. Once these names, written on cards, have been sorted into the four piles, Giffin goes out and corrals the first tournament player he can find and brings him back to the PGA office. This player then shuffles each group of cards separately and sorts it into piles of three. The result is the pairings for the opening 36 holes of play. Thus tournament winners are paired with tournament winners, big check winners with big check winners, and so on. After the first two rounds the pairings become even more automatic. Players with similar scores are grouped together in threesomes, like this: the tournament leader is paired with the player in third and the player in fifth. Second place is paired with fourth and sixth. This formula operates all the way down the line.

For the first two rounds, at least, the outstanding players are thus always grouped together. A dew sweeper or Ghost Squadron member will have to shoot two good rounds early in the tournament before he can be paired with the big guns. Thus the written caste system sets up the unwritten one. Not only does winning a tournament give you status on the tour, it also throws you in with the name performers as far as starting times are concerned. You have thus graduated from the Dew Sweepers, Litter Brigade or Ghost Squadron and earned a certain amount of respect within your own profession. It is also a way of widening your range of friendships.

Until this happens, however, most rookies keep pretty much to themselves. No one would walk out for a practice round, throw his clubs down on the first tee and say to Julius Boros or Sam Snead or Arnold Palmer: "Hi, Arnie, Jay, how about a round of golf?" First of all, his reception would be a frosty one to say the least. Secondly, most players have their own little groups, their own games, their money games, their practice games. They are not about to take in a newcomer even if he isn't as brash as a burglar.

There is one glaring exception to this policy. When Jerry Barber first came out on the tour in 1948, he deliberately set out to crash the cliques formed by some of the top players, but he had a pretty sharp reason for doing so and an excellent way of going about it. He managed to play practice rounds with the likes of Snead, Hogan and Lloyd Mangrum by offering to play for the same high stakes. At first he was a consistent loser, but since it seemed such a profitable venture the players he lost to were perfectly willing to keep playing with him. By this process Barber learned some of the tricks of professional tournament golf from its masters. He figured his gambling losses were just another method of paying for an education. It wasn't long before his education was so solid that he began to win some of that tuition back.

Even Barber would not have dared to tamper with some of the other protocols of the pro tour. Until a player is a top money winner himself he will not, for instance, sit down in the clubhouse grillroom with the top players even if there is plenty of room at the table. He will never walk out to the practice tee when it is crowded and push right in, saying to one of the stars, "How about moving over? I'd like to practice here and I'm a little late and I just need to hit a few balls to warm up and how about letting me use a few of yours?" This happens all the time between close friends. Out on the practice tee there is a lot of pushing and kidding, either about yesterday's round or the one coming up. The rookies usually don't take part in this, however, even among themselves.

The way to beat the circuit's caste system, if you don't want to be a lone wolf, is to seek out members of your own caste, especially those who have been around just a bit longer than you have. I was lucky to fall in with three very congenial men, dark-haired Johnny Pott, who had played golf at Louisiana State University and gone right from the campus to the tour in 1957; slender Tommy Jacobs, who had won the National Junior championship in 1951 and had gone on the tour in 1957; and muscular Jim Ferree, a lively, talkative North Carolinian who had been on the tour since 1956. For most of the year we traveled together, lived together, ate together, went out together and played our practice rounds together.

Together we formed a buffer of sorts against the hard life of the tour. Our group held ranks pretty well until late in 1958 when Ferree and Jacobs won their first tournaments and greatly expanded their sphere of activities. We were still friends, but their lives had changed rather radically while Johnny and I remained behind treading water.

Several tangible things happen to the player who wins his first tournament. If he has already made business connections, he will receive several thousand dollars in bonuses. If he has not he will now be swamped with offers. First of all, he can deal from strength with equipment manufacturers who may want him to use their equipment exclusively on the tour. This will involve free clubs and balls plus an annual salary of $1000 to $5000 to a young, only moderately distinguished player. He can now also sign with clothing and shoe manufacturers for small bonuses and all the shoes, slacks and shirts he can wear. Conventional country clubs, in addition to resort or real estate developments, will be after him to join their professional staffs. This practice has created the odd expression "playing out of." It means nothing more than that a touring pro will pay one or two short visits to a club and sign the club's name after his name when he registers for a golf tournament. In return, he will pull down an annual fee of $1500 to $10,000. Thus a golf fan will often read in the paper that Jack Nicklaus, who really lives in Columbus, Ohio, is suddenly signing up as coming from Tucson, Arizona; that Jim Ferree of North Carolina is now from Corona, California; that Billy Maxwell of Dallas, Texas, is suddenly from Las Vegas, Nevada; that Paul Harney of Worcester, Massachusetts, is suddenly from Sacramento, California; Mike Souchak of Durham, North Carolina, is from Grossingers, New York; Jack Burke of Houston, is from Kiamesha Lake, New York; Dow Finsterwald of Athens, Ohio, is from Tequesta, Florida; Doug Sanders of Cedartown, Georgia, is from Ojai, California, and Joe Campbell of Nashville, Tennessee, once registered out of the Little Club in New York City. South Africa's Gary Player registered for a while as coming from Langhorne, Pennsylvania, without once setting foot in the town. These designations change from year to year and month to month.

Business agents pursue the new winners like hounds after a fox, but the intangible values of winning his first tournament are often even more profitable to the young pro. In that given week he has proved to everyone, but most of all to himself, that he is capable of beating the best, that he belongs where he is. The confidence this supplies to the winner is limitless and, conversely, the feeling of insecurity and frustration that begins to build in the player who somehow can't seem to grab off his first title is likewise limitless. We were happy for them, of course, but Johnny Pott and I looked on enviously as Tommy Jacobs and Jim Ferree were pulled into a richer and faster orbit.

Actually, of our group, I was the first one to come close to winning a tournament, and it was a frightening experience. This was during the sixth week of the 1958 winter tour and the troupe had settled in Tucson. The El Rio Country Club, where we were playing, is a flat desert course with numerous desert palms and scrub pines lining the fairways. It is a good course but fairly short and not too difficult. I shot a 63 to take second in the pre-tournament pro-am event and then scored a 66 in the first round and a 65 in the second. This was pretty exceptional golf, and my score of 131 for 36 holes put me into a tie for first place with a veteran player from Provo, Utah, named Bill Johnston. On the third day I played badly — in my early years on the tour I could always produce at least one bad round a tournament — but managed to score and even par 70. Most of the leaders were shooting rounds in the 60's, but I was still in pretty good shape. My score for 54 holes was 201 and I was in a tie for third place, three shots behind leader Don January; I thought to myself, "You played poorly and still shot a 70. You have an excellent chance to win."

Up to this time I had played in a fair number of big tournaments, ten of them to be exact, not counting the minor Imperial Valley Open which I had won. I had done pretty well in a couple of them, but this was the first in which I had a real chance to win — the first time I experienced the terrors of real pressure and how it can affect a man. I was in a brand-new situation and I simply didn't know how to react to it. The result was that I went to pieces.

I was in bed early the night before the final round, but I hardly slept at all. I had strange, fitful dreams and then lay awake most of the night worrying about the oddest thing. I was trying to figure out what I would say at the presentation ceremony. I finally dropped off to sleep around 4 A.M.

Even with little sleep I still felt pretty good the following day. That is, until the pressure hit me like a sudden electric shock on the first hole. I was paired with the leader, January, and an old-timer named John Barnum, who was in fifth, just a stroke behind me. On the first hole I hit a nice drive well down the fairway and had nothing but a short 9-iron shot left to the green. I felt a little shaky by now and I didn't quite catch the ball solidly and left it about 18 or 20 feet short of the cup. I putted first and rolled the ball up to within two feet. I then marked the ball with a dime, picked the ball up and stepped back to let the others hit their putts. As I stood there waiting I could feel myself tightening up, my knees feeling a little wobbly, my breath coming in fast, quick spurts, the way it does when you jump into a very cold lake or ocean and try to swim. By the time I got over my short putt I really had the shakes. I didn't even get the ball anywhere near the hole from two feet.

After that I didn't have a chance. The holes are all short ones, but suddenly they all began to look so difficult. Suddenly every hazard on the course jumped out at me like a flashing neon light. The fairways that seemed so wide the preceding three days now looked like narrow little paths through fields of wheat. Trouble seemed everywhere and soon I didn't even feel as if it was me swinging the club. I got several strokes over par, completely out of the tournament, and finally just began to swing away with sheer abandon, not caring whether I made a bogey or a birdie and usually getting one or the other. I birdied the last hole for a 75, a score of 276 and a tie for fourteenth place, 11 shots back of winner Lionel Hebert.

It was my first experience with choking up and I began to think that if that kind of physical reaction set in every time I was in contention I would be a pretty sorry mess — either because my nerves would explode like firecrackers if it happened a couple of more times or because I would never be in contention again. Either alternative seemed pretty dismal. It was an experience that stayed with me for a long, long time, until winning that first tournament began to seem like finding the pot of gold at the end of the rainbow. It is not much consolation to think that this kind of emotional upheaval has bothered other players as well. Don January summed it up very well after he lost the 1961 PGA championship in a play-off with Jerry Barber. The winner had caught him on the last three regulation holes with putts of 20, 40 and 60 feet, but January had had a couple of chances to wrap it up, in spite of Barber's phenomenal putting, and had missed them both. "I guess I was just plain scared to win that dude," was his unique and colorful way of expressing a pretty common state of mind.

Another discovery I made in those early months was that there were several ways to blow tournaments even while keeping one's nervous system under control. At the Azalea Open in March I was in sixth place after two rounds, but finished 76–76 and tumbled to sixteenth. Lema blows again? No. Just a bad case of the flu.

At Greensboro in April I thought I was going to win the tournament even as I stood on the last green of the last round. Art Wall, who was playing with me, needed to sink a 15-foot putt to tie and Sam Snead, playing just behind us, needed to birdie the last hole to tie. While Wall was lining up his putt, I strolled over to the scorer's table by the edge of the green wearing a mood of confidence as if it were a brand-new alpaca sweater. There I was informed not only that Don January had finished with a sizzling 64 that tied me, but that Bob Goalby had shot a 66 and would certainly win the tournament by at least two shots. To accentuate the negative, Wall made his 15-foot putt, Snead made his birdie, and we all finished in a five-way tie for second. Moral? You can shoot great golf and still get beaten.

A week later South Africa's Gary Player won his first tournament in the United States and I was almost glad. Except that I wished it had happened some other way. We were playing in the Kentucky Derby Open in Louisville (a misnomer, because the Derby was not scheduled to be run off for another two weeks) and Gary and I were driving back and forth to the course each day together. He kept up a stream of amusing talk about how grateful he was to be able to play on the U.S. tour, what he hoped to learn from the U.S. players and how much he enjoyed the whole experience. He certainly has enjoyed the whole experience. He has won our Masters, our PGA and several other tournaments and has probably taught us more about the game than we could ever hope to teach him.

That week I got a very special kind of lesson, however, that only experience can thoroughly teach. We were playing on a rock-hard, exceptionally hilly public course, the Seneca Country Club, and it was a very hot week even for Louisville. I was pretty hot, too. I started the tournament with a pair of 67's and was tied for the lead at the halfway point with Paul Harney. Leading a tournament can be fun as well as tense. You are up there on top, the newspapers are full of you, and the other players have always got the friendly needle out. "Hail Our Leader," they are likely to say. "Feel like choking a little bit today?"

For once I didn't choke, but for a while I would have been happy to have drowned. Johnny Pott and I had been paired together for the first two rounds, and after the second round, which we had finished early in the afternoon, we stopped at a drive-in for lunch on the way to the motel and then spent three hours in the motel swimming pool. Pott just lounged around the edge of the pool, eying the girls pretty carefully, while I decided to show off with a long and vigorous exhibition of swimming and diving. I didn't feel anything at the time, but the next morning when I tried to swing a golf club my arms felt like two bags of sand. They were not stiff or sore, they just felt as if they must have belonged to some other player in the tournament. In the third round, therefore, I was lucky to bring home a 75. The following day I had to birdie three of the last four holes to post a 72-hole score of 279 and a tie for sixth. Moral? Swimming is for beach boys, not for golfers.

So my rookie year rolled on. In June I learned the pleasurable lesson that winning golf and late dating seldom go together. The tour had hit New York for the $50,000 Pepsi-Cola Open on Long Island and it was my first visit to this huge, busy city. As soon as I hit town I called up a girl I had been pretty fond of back home and who had become a successful New York model. She showed me every lively spot in town, and if I had a late tee-off time I simply stayed over in the city. The golf course was just a place I was forced to spend four or five hours each day away from this beautifully built female. My scores were even higher than the tabs I was picking up each night and I finally finished 17 shots back of winner Arnold Palmer. I was lucky and placed well enough to earn $150, but my check didn't even cover two nights on the town.

There were some good times for the rest of the group, too. At least on the golf course. In September both Ferree and Jacobs scored their first victories. The tour stopped in British Columbia in very late August for the $40,000 Vancouver Open and the four of us — Jacobs, Pott, Ferree and myself — took an apartment in a lush apartment hotel called the Georgian Towers. We were a big crowd for one apartment, but after a few days Pott and Ferree managed to get a suite of their own in the same building.

The golf course was well laid out but not too difficult a challenge. With a little luck you could shoot some pretty low scores on it. Jim started out with a 69, a shot off the lead, and then in the second round fired a fantastic 11 under par 61 that put him out front to stay. The tournament had started on a Thursday, and because no professional sports were permitted on Sunday, the players were taken on a pleasure cruise up the Strait of Georgia after the third round. This put a lot of pressure on Jim, sitting on his lead all day like that with nothing to do but ride around in a boat. The rest of us were afraid he might blow the tournament, but Jim is such an easygoing, extroverted fellow that the pressure never really did get to him until he had such a big lead it didn't matter.

It had been a long time in coming. "This is like pouring water down a dry well," he said at the presentation ceremonies. Jim made a huge hit with the galleries and the tournament sponsors in Vancouver. Throughout the tournament he had worn a tiny, crazy-looking straw hat. The club kept the hat after he had left and made a bronze replica of it for display in their trophy case.

Then two weeks later Tommy Jacobs won *his* first tournament. Tommy is a very intense person who smokes a great deal, at least a pack during an 18-hole round and probably two or three packs during the entire day. We were playing in the Denver Centennial, in the town that Tommy was raised in, and the two of us roomed together again that week in a little motel on the outskirts. Tom shot a 65 the first day and took a lead he too held right to the end of the tournament. Leading all the way like this can be hard on a tournament golfer's nerves, because you have the feeling you're sitting up there alone and everyone is shooting at you. If you win the tournament, well, you were leading, weren't you? If you lose the tournament the thought persists, especially in your own mind, that you blew it.

In a case like this the leader's roommate must show special consideration. If he wants a Coke you run and fetch him a Coke. If he feels a little nervous you tell him how great he is playing, that he has nothing to worry about, that no one else has a chance, all he has to do is to keep doing the things he has been doing. You give the fellow a real snow job. Often it's stuff he doesn't really believe or even want to hear, but it seems to work pretty well.

The night before the last round Tommy and I went out to dinner with some Denver friends of his and on the way back to our motel the car broke down. It was about 11 o'clock at night and here we were climbing all over the stubborn automobile. The fan belt or something had busted. Tommy was down under the hood and I was lying on the engine as if the car had swallowed me up. We were hammering away at this blasted car with wrenches, hammers and screwdrivers and we were both covered with grease and dirt just as if we didn't have to go out the next day and play in a golf tournament that Tommy had such a great chance to win. We finally got the thing fixed and went to bed about 1 A.M. We talked a little bit before dropping off to sleep and I was surprised to see how little Tommy was reacting to the pressure. Then the next morning I woke up early and looked over at him. The ashtray on the side of his bed was so crammed with cigarette butts it looked like a plateful of noodles. So he had been feeling the pressure. On the course, however, his nerves are terrific. A bunch of guys the final day were shooting 64's and 65's, but Tom scored his third straight 67 and won by a shot. Now he too was gone from the Dew Sweepers and Litter Brigade.

My year ended well enough, too. I was among the top forty money winners and therefore was invited to play in two rich tournaments in Havana during November. I finished fourth and sixth in the two events, and all of us were given the red carpet treatment — free rooms at the best hotels, chauffeured limousines, cocktail parties at private haciendas. I was getting a taste of being an international playboy and it seemed pretty intoxicating to a rookie on the pro tour. It was a long way from the canneries of Oakland, the pro shop at the San Francisco Golf Club or the little nine-hole municipal golf course in Elko, Nevada. When I returned home for the Christmas holidays I was pretty pleased with myself. I had won over $10,000 in official money, a few thousand more in unofficial money at pro-ams, and I was looking forward to a much better year in 1959. I felt that all I needed to do was make a few minor alterations in my game and I would not only win my first tournament, I would win a lot of tournaments. Jacobs and Ferree had done it. Now I would do it.

The changes I wanted to make were simple ones. I decided that I needed to hit the ball on a higher trajectory and with a left to right fade. I felt this was necessary because we played so many elevated and heavily trapped greens that I wanted to bring the ball into them with a high flight. The ball would thus clear the danger in front of the green and also land with the soft impact that a fading ball achieves. I had the right idea, but I was going about it in the wrong way. I had a good swing and a good grip, but to develop the new trajectory I tried to change my grip. What I should have done was simply move the ball farther to the left at address and stayed down with the shot longer at impact.

These adjustments were going to make me a big winner, a top star, a rich man. As it turned out they almost put me out of business entirely.

# 6 / *Whatever happened to . . . ?*

A CLOSE look at the scoring averages on the golf tour reveals what a narrow margin separates the big winners like Arnold Palmer, Jack Nicklaus, Julius Boros or Gary Player from the also-rans. It is usually as little as a stroke per 18 holes. In 1963 Palmer averaged 70.63 shots for every round he played (he played 79) and won seven tournaments and $128,000. Fred Hawkins played in ten more tournaments than Palmer, but did not win a single one, earned only $25,000 (which placed him twenty-third on the money list) and yet his stroke-per-round average was 71.72, one shot, one missed putt per 18 holes behind Arnold!

Does this mean that Fred Hawkins could become an Arnold Palmer if he could improve his score by an average of one stroke a round? Not exactly, but he could come awfully close. This narrow margin is an endless source of encouragement to the also-rans who know that if they can improve just an iota they too can be big winners. This narrow margin, conversely, is small comfort to the players on top. Take just a slight edge off a champion's game and he is suddenly back with the pack. That is why it is impossible to look at a group of ten golfers and predict which one will come out the best in the long run. We look at Palmer winning tournament after tournament and we say that he has a much more effective swing than Jack Belsey's. If Jack Belsey suddenly started to win — and this kind of thing is not inconceivable — we would immediately begin to see all the things in Belsey's swing that made him such a great player.

When Billy Casper first came out on the tour in 1955 an authoritative prediction was made by one of the tour's most successful players. "Billy Casper won't last more than six months on the tour," he said. "All he can do is putt." Here was a guy who knew the game of golf very well and that was the best he could do in calling the turn on Billy Casper, currently one of the best putters from 400 yards in to the hole that the tour has ever seen. This prominent player isn't even on the tour anymore. He gave Casper six months, but he would have been quite accurate, it turned out, if he had applied the deadline to himself.

If you examine the swings that many of the successful players use you might well decide that not one of them is any good. Palmer lunges at the ball and punches it. Nicklaus has the unorthodox habit of letting his right elbow fly far out from his body as he takes the club back. Jacky Cupit has such a loop at the top of his backswing that it makes him look as if he were waving a flag. I myself loop noticeably at the top. Billy Maxwell leaps at the ball like a panhandler diving for a ten-spot. Julius Boros is all hands and wrists like a man dusting the furniture. Jerry Barber has his wrists completely cocked practically before he has even started his swing. Doug Sanders braces himself with a wide stance that looks like a sailor leaning into a northeast gale and takes the club back barely far enough to get it off the ground. If you lined these eight players up on the practice tee without knowing who in the world they were and asked them to hit a few shots your advice would be simple: "Go back home and sell insurance.

You haven't got it." Yet here they are, the top players in the game.

No player, with the possible exception of Sam Snead, has the kind of swing that is going to guarantee success. It is the ability to make it repeat itself everytime that counts. Also vitally important is the intangible that I have stressed so strongly earlier: the emotional approach to the game. It is undoubtedly a weakness in that department that will suddenly reduce a Ralph Guldahl, who won the U.S. Open two years running, in 1936 and 1937, from headliner to hacker. It partly explains why my game suddenly went to pot for two lean years and it almost totally explains what happened to two of the players on the current tour who at one time were almost universally believed to be the successors to Hogan and Snead. They both were on the verge of winning every major championship in sight and becoming the kind of star that Palmer and Nicklaus have turned out to be. It is ironic that at one time when fine golf swings were being talked about the names of Mike Souchak and Ken Venturi were invariably mentioned. Their sudden declines are worth looking at in an attempt to explain why this kind of thing happens.

Mike Souchak is a burly, gregarious character who works pretty hard on his golf, but is like me in believing that life should be fun as well as productive. He was an all-conference end and place-kicker on the Duke football team in the late 1940's. He's about five feet ten inches tall, weighs over two hundred pounds and has the thick, solid neck that identifies the contact sport athlete. He probably would have made a better than average professional in that sport as well. But Mike became addicted to golf on the Duke golf team and became a professional when he got out of school. Mike would probably have made a pretty good politician too, because he has an uncanny memory for names. He will sometimes be on the putting green, look up to see a face he hasn't seen for three years and then only briefly. "Hi there, Ralph," he'll say without a moment's hesitation while Ralph, or whoever it is, will stand there with an incredulous expression on his face, scarcely believing what his ears have heard. Most of us are obliged to resort to dodges like, "Hi there, Tiger," or "Whattaya say, pro?"

Souchak came on the tour in 1953 and by 1955 he was performing brilliantly. That was the year he won the Texas Open at Brackenridge Park in San Antonio, setting or tying three PGA scoring records in the process. His first round of 60 tied the 18-hole mark. He also fired a 27 for the first nine holes that day, still a PGA record, and a four-day total of 257, also the current record. Just to show that this was no fluke he won the Houston Open the very next week, then finished out the year by winning the Havana Invitational and making fourth place on the overall money winning list with a total of $29,462, terrifically good money in those days. The next year really established Mike as a top star. He won four tournaments, including the very tough Colonial National Invitation tournament at Fort Worth. That was the year I saw him getting a haircut during the U.S. Open in Rochester and felt as if I were brushing elbows with immortality.

The greatest year Mike had was probably 1959. He was hitting the ball farther than anyone on the tour with the exception of George Bayer, and he was hitting it straight. It began to look as if he would tear every tournament to pieces. Arnold Palmer had already won his first Masters the year before, but in 1959 he didn't look nearly as good as Mike Souchak on the crest of his wave. In April he won the Tournament of Champions at Las Vegas. In June he almost won the U.S.

Open, but bogeyed the last hole when he needed a birdie to tie Billy Casper and therefore finished in third, two shots back. In July he won the Western Open, beating Palmer by a shot, and when in August Souchak won the Motor City Open he apparently felt he'd accomplished enough for one year and dropped off the tour. He did come back for two tournaments in the fall, but he passed up nine of the last eleven events.

Most of the players on the tour were a bit relieved, but very, very surprised when Mike retired with so much of the season still unplayed. When a player gets a hot hand such as Mike had that summer it is usually considered smart to stay with it until excess fatigue begins to cool off the hot streak. That is the way you win money, tournament titles, and bank confidence for drawing on in the future. Take my case for example. I had pretty well played myself out in the fall of '62 when I suddenly broke through to win the Sahara Invitational. Even though I was dog tired I stayed on because I was playing fine golf and I wasn't about to squander a hot streak lying around on a beach somewhere. The result was that three weeks later I won my first official PGA tournament, won another shortly thereafter and closed out the year by winning the Mexican Open. The confidence I gained in that stretch carried right into the next season and in part made possible my very good year of 1963.

Whether Mike would have gained the necessary confidence to start winning major championships like the Masters, the Open, or the PGA is just guesswork. It is a fact, however, that he had had only average years — poor ones for Mike — in 1957 and 1958, winning only one tournament and a two-year total of $36,000. It is also a fact that, in addition to coming close at the Open, he came very close to winning the PGA Championship. A bad final round by Mike (74) and a sensational

[ 83 ]

one by Bob Rosburg (66) knocked him out of it. It is my feeling that really sticking with it in 1959 might have brought Mike through to the major championships. It might have prevented the cruel setback that struck him in the Open in Denver the following year.

The U.S. Open of 1960 was played at the Cherry Hills Country Club, in a southern suburb of Denver. The course is not too long, about 6800 yards, and the high altitude and thin air make it possible to hit the ball about 10 percent farther than on a sea-level course. Mike started out like the Mike of 1959. He burned red-hot during the first two rounds, shooting scores of 68 and 67 to set an Open record at 36 holes of 135. At that point he led the tournament by three strokes over Doug Sanders and five over the rest of the field. He continued to play well on the morning of the final day and came to the last tee of the third round with a chance to hold a four-shot lead starting off after lunch. A four-shot lead with only 18 holes left to play is golden. It gives the leader a chance to play almost anyway he wants to. It forces the players behind him to gamble in the hopes that they can cut the margin. At the U.S. Open it is a dangerous thing to gamble.

There was Mike on the eighteenth tee that morning with the Open as good as his. Then, just as he reached the top of his backswing a camera, aimed by one of the spectators in the gallery behind him, clicked loudly in the silence. Startled, Mike hooked his drive into the pond that stretches out in front of the eighteenth tee at Cherry Hills. It cost him two strokes and he carried a two-shot lead, not a four-shot margin, into the final round that afternoon. Mike's game sagged and he shot a 75, while Arnold Palmer was shooting a 65 to win the tournament.

A couple of weeks later at another tournament Mike and I

ate dinner together and I asked him, as one golfer who had
blown tournaments to another: "What happened to you at
Denver?"

"I guess it just wasn't meant to be my day," was what he
said. "All afternoon I kept thinking about that camera clicking, about the two strokes I had lost on account of it, and
about what those two strokes could mean. I just never was
able to concentrate on what I should have been doing."

Mike Souchak is a tragic reverse example of what the Open
does and could mean to a golfer. Because he combines a
cheerful spirit with a big tee shot Mike has always been extremely popular with the people who follow golf. He has
won plenty of tournaments and still takes about $50,000 a
year from various sources out of the game, but an Open title
for Mike could mean an extra $150,000 to $300,000 a year in
outside deals. He knows this as well as anyone and Mike's
tragedy is that he has come so close so often without winning.
Palmer has won the British Open and the Masters, but winning the U.S. Open the year Mike had all but won it is what
has put Arnold over the top and made him the great public
hero he is today. Winning could well have done the same
for Souchak.

After his close call at Denver, Souchak's career began to
taper off. He won the Buick Open shortly afterward and finished the year as sixth leading money winner with $29,000.
He had a chance to win the Open again in 1961, but was
weakened by a virus and shot a last-round 73 that put him in
fourth, three shots back of winner Gene Littler. Since then
he has dropped far down the money winning list. He was
twenty-eighth in 1961, twenty-ninth in 1962 and fifty-third in
1963. I've heard Mike say that he's been on the tour a long
time now, that he's made a lot of sacrifices, leaving his wife

and children at home while he disappears onto the tour for weeks at a time, and that he's fed up with making any more sacrifices. That's only partly it. Mike likes to step up to the bar and take a drink in convivial company and he's not about to stay in his motel and watch television if he can have dinner in one of the town's best restaurants. But I also think that what Mike is going through now is something he can't really understand. It happens to a lot of the tour's good players. Mike established himself as a winner pretty quickly. He had tremendous natural talent and all the confidence in the world. Once he started to win he began to get a few outside things going for him, like exhibitions, a better contract with the equipment manufacturer he was tied in with, things that made the tour less of a struggle. He was in demand for every kind of appearance: business, publicity and just plain social. I'm sure it began to take his mind off his golf and he began to ease off a little, at least in the sense that he couldn't stay fired up every week. I have known this feeling, even in the years when I was trying so hard to win my first title. A player may have won his share of tournaments and then one week he is not playing too well — it's hard work just to get somewhere in the money — and he says, "What the hell, chalk it up to a bad week. I'll be back on the stick next time." I'm not saying this is always a conscious decision. Very often it is unconscious. He knows it is happening to him, but there is nothing he can or even wants to do about it.

The next step is often a prolonged slump. This is usually brought on because he has been playing carelessly and has fallen into some bad habits. Then little things like missed putts, bad bounces on the fairway or green, or gallery noises begin to disturb him way out of proportion to their usual ability to annoy. I played with Souchak a few times last year and his putting, he would say, was not sharp. Well, it might not have been, but as soon as he missed a couple of makable putts on the early holes he began fighting what he thought to be an uphill struggle. This is a mental slump. When he was winning nothing bothered him; now everything does.

Having to leave his family at home while he plays the tour is one of the big things that bothers Mike. The tour can be a lonely profession even when you are playing well. When you arc playing badly it is like solitary confinement on Devil's Island. The solution to this is not obvious, even if the kids are not in school and you can afford to have your family with you on tour. Tommy Jacobs loves his wife and children certainly as much as anyone out here. He'd like to have them with him, but he has also discovered that while his mental frame of mind improves when they are traveling with him, physically he deteriorates. The kids are young, have odd sleeping hours and the strain put on the whole crowd — his wife Sally especially — by Tommy's competitive schedule of playing early one day and late the next, is hard to stand. As much as he hates to do it Tommy leaves the family at home in their house by the Bermuda Dunes golf course in Palm Springs, California, and returns home whenever separation becomes unbearable.

The vacation at home isn't always restful either. After the PGA Championship in Dallas last July I had a long talk with Johnny Pott. I had played badly in the tournament, but had a great deal of luck and finished tied for thirteenth. John had played badly, but had no luck at all and missed the 36-hole cutdown. His nerves weren't too good and his morale was pretty low. He was going back home to Mississippi, to his wife and two kids, and to the family-run Gulf Hills golf course, for a long vacation. He planned to stay there until well into

September and I advised him not even to look at a club for the first week or so he was home.

Three weeks later my wife Betty and I were in Hartford for the Insurance City Open. A couple of nights before the tournament started we ate dinner at a German restaurant across the street from the Statler Hilton Hotel. I was just cutting into my steak when I heard a familiar voice behind me.

"Well, hello you honeymooners," Johnny Pott said.

"If it isn't the old married man," I said. "Greetings. I thought you were home for a long rest."

"Oh, man," John said with a laugh. "Mary Rose worked me so hard at home that I had to come back out on the tour to get my health back."

Mary Rose couldn't have worked him too hard and the visit with his family certainly must have done a lot of good. The next week John snapped out of a yearlong slump by winning one of the toughest tournaments of the year, the American Golf Classic on the very long Firestone golf course in Akron.

What all this means is that the problem is a pretty typical and common one. Up until the late 1950's the tourists with children used to buy trailers and bring the entire family along. When Gary Player lived in South Africa he used to keep his wife and three kids on tour with him and hired a traveling governess to keep the situation under control. This must have cost him between $600 and $800 a week and even prosperous young Gary couldn't afford that for long. He now has a tie-up with Huntington Hartford's new course on Paradise Island in the Bahamas and the family lives there. It is so convenient to the States that Gary can get home for frequent visits. A lot of the younger married players drive from tournament to tournament with the family, put up in motels and pay the price, both in money and the energy it takes to run a family on the road. Some of the successful ones, like Palmer, Player and Nicklaus, will fly their wives out to many of the tournaments and leave the kids back home. In any case it can get to be a severe problem, both for the golfers and their wives and families. Considering the built-in strain it is surprising how few golfing families break up.

So you see there are more reasons behind a slump than a bad swing or a jerky putting rhythm. All you have to do is lose that one or two strokes somewhere over the long, arduous course of a 72-hole tournament, and you are completely out of contention. In Souchak's case I think the eventual outcome will be another return to the great form he showed in 1959. At thirty-seven a man with his great talent for golf, a man who has come so close to smelling genuine, big-time success, isn't going to let it get away without a good, vigorous battle. He has worked very hard on his game and I think has made up his mind that whatever the cost he will get as much out of himself as he possibly can. Where Mike is concerned this is a great deal. If he starts winning major championships he has it in him to become one of the great sports figures of his time.

An even more startling example of a golfer reaching the edge of greatness and then suddenly dropping back into obscurity is that supplied by high-strung Ken Venturi. The sudden collapse of Ken's career is one of the tragedies of the pro tour, but his efforts to regain the form that suddenly deserted him in late 1960 have provided a clear, undiluted case history of courage.

For several years before he turned pro in 1957 Venturi was the top amateur on the West Coast and one of the best in the country. He was the big name around San Francisco when I was first breaking into the game. He started out as a public course player who hit the ball with a big publinks-type hook. He played in the national public links championship a couple of times and won the California Amateur a couple of times too. Then he came under the eye of Eddie Lowery, the Lincoln-Mercury dealer from San Francisco who has helped me and other players out from time to time. Lowery sent him to former U.S. Open and Masters champion Byron Nelson for a series of lessons. Nelson taught him to hit the ball straight and swing with the perfect balance of a gymnast. In fact, when Ken was playing well a few years ago, his balance, from the start to the finish of his swing, was something special. One can admire Hogan's swing for its efficiency and Snead's swing for its natural beauty and perfection, but Venturi's swing seemed like an ideal blend of the two. Ken stood up to the ball as if he, the golf club, the ball and the golf course were all part of a beautiful piece of sculpture. He looked like a great boxer, someone like Sugar Ray Robinson, ready to dance in on an opponent.

Ken made the Walker Cup team in 1953 and the following spring played in his first Masters. He was only a twenty-two-year-old amateur at the time but he tied for sixteenth place along with such notables as Julius Boros, Jay Hebert and Australia's Peter Thomson. From then on Ken was in love with the Masters. He dreamed about playing in it, he dreamed about winning it. He was in love with the tournament and the golf course.

In 1956, after a year with the Army overseas in Germany, Ken came back to Augusta again. The Masters is an exclusive invitational tournament. A player has to earn his way into it or be voted in by past Masters, Open or Amateur champions. Ken got in for the 1956 by a vote of the former Masters champions. I understand there was quite a bit of lobbying by

Nelson and Lowery to see that he got the votes. It didn't take long for Ken to prove that he had earned them because that year he almost became a Masters champion himself. For three days he stood the tournament on its ear. For three days every golf fan in the United States followed the tournament with unabated excitement as this amateur led the world's best pros. Going into the final day Venturi had produced rounds of 66, 69, and 75 and led the field by four full shots. Then came the first of two tragedies.

The final day was very windy. This meant that the ball was hard to control in the air, of course, but the wind also dried out the greens so thoroughly that they became as slick as a dance floor. Up until that time it had been something of a Masters tradition to pair Byron Nelson on the last day with the 54-hole leader. Ken was leading the tournament at that point and no doubt looked forward to the prospect of playing this crucial round of golf with his friend and adviser. Nelson would not be able to give him any advice during the round, of course; that is a violation of the rules of golf and means disqualification for the player who willingly accepts it. But Nelson would certainly have had a soothing effect on Ken, who is emotional under any circumstances let alone leading one of the world's most important golf tournaments. In this case the two gentlemen who run the Masters tournament with such efficiency — Cliff Roberts, the New York banker, and Bobby Jones, the great golfer from Atlanta — felt that it would not really be proper to have the tournament leader playing with the man who taught him the game. So instead of pairing Venturi with Nelson they sent the young amateur out with the veteran Sam Snead. I've played with Sam quite a few times during my years on the tour and I have always enjoyed observing his skill at such close quarters. But during a round of golf Sam tends to be a little on the dour side. He doesn't smile much, or comment about your good shots. He's a pretty serious competitor.

On this windy Sunday afternoon of April 8, 1956, Ken was certainly bothered more by the wind than by the fact that he was playing with Snead. He felt a little disappointed at not being able to play with Nelson, but he worked hard all the way around and finally staggered in with an 80. When Jack Burke, playing out in front of him, shot a 71, Ken was beaten by a shot. Burke had made up an eight-stroke deficit to do it.

Ken had created a lot of excitement, among golfers and non-golfers alike, in making his great bid to be the first amateur ever to win the Masters. When it was over a lot of people accused Ken, though not to his face, of taking the gas and blowing the tournament. Not Snead though.

"Ken didn't blow the tournament," Snead said. "He just had a lot of trouble trying to figure out those real slick greens. The wind was bad and after he'd miss the green with his approach shot it made it awful hard to get a par because the little short putts he needed never seemed to break the way he thought they would."

All you have to do is look at a record book to show that Sam was right and that a lot of other players were having trouble the last day too. Mike Souchak, who was playing with Burke, also shot an 80. So did Julius Boros, Nelson himself and Chick Harbert. Jimmy Demaret, who'd won the Masters three times, shot an 81. So did Jack Fleck and Jay Hebert. Ted Kroll shot an 82, Lionel Hebert had an 83, Fred Hawkins had an 84 and Don Fairfield took 86 blows. There were even higher scores — an amateur named Charlie Kunkle from Johnstown, Pennsylvania, had a 95 — and it is unfair to describe the 1956 Masters as the one Ken Venturi blew. The fact that the winner shot 71 on a day the world's best pros had trouble breaking 80, makes it the Masters that Jack Burke won.

So that was Ken's first cruel setback in the tournament he cares so much about. He came so close and had the victory snatched away from him at the last moment. After that, winning at Augusta became an obsession with Ken. He turned pro in the fall of 1956 and joined the tour the following year. He was an instant success. In those days you couldn't start winning prize money on the tour until six months after you had filed your application with the PGA. Ken therefore didn't become eligible to really start collecting until the end of May, but in his rookie year he still pocketed almost $19,000. He also won back-to-back tournaments at St. Paul and Milwaukee. He played in the Masters again in 1957 and finished twelfth. In 1958 he tied for fourth in the Masters, just two shots back of winner Arnold Palmer, and went on to win three tournaments that year. Ken was playing so well week after week that he became the favorite at every tournament he entered. Pretty soon he was going to start winning his share of major titles.

It looked as if 1960 would be the year. Palmer had not yet started to dominate professional golf the way he has in recent years. Somber Art Wall had been the leading money winner in 1959 and had won the Masters as well, but Wall was ailing in 1960. The top players were Venturi, Palmer, poker-faced Gene Littler, Dow Finsterwald, who was making big money playing careful, percentage golf, Billy Casper, the great putter who had won the 1959 U.S. Open, and Mike Souchak, who had had such a fine year in 1959, before he went on his long vacation. Then came the 1960 Masters.

Palmer started out in that tournament with a 67 to Venturi's 73, but by the start of the final round Ken had cut Palmer's

lead to one shot and he was tied for second place with Finsterwald, Casper, Julius Boros, and Ben Hogan. Playing head-to-
head with Finsterwald on the final day and a few holes in
front of Palmer, Ken turned in a fine two under par 70 for a
final score of 283, one shot ahead of Dow and apparently out
of reach of Palmer, who faced the difficult task of having to
birdie the last two holes in order to win.

Ken finished his round in high excitement. He was half
carried, half pulled into Cliff Robert's private quarters in the
Augusta National's rambling white Georgian colonial clubhouse. He was being pounded on the back, cheered and congratulated. It seemed impossible for anyone to catch him.
Ken had the feeling deep inside of him, right then and there,
that he had finally won the tournament he had worked so
diligently to win, had pointed for through long hours of practice. He had finally arrived as a star of the first magnitude.
Venturi was given a seat in front of a television set, along
with Roberts and Jones, to watch Palmer's finish. What he
saw was so heartbreaking and so shocking that it sent tears
streaming down his face. On the seventeenth, as most golfers
have committed to memory by now, he saw Palmer barely
reach the green with his approach shot and then pound in a
30-foot putt to birdie that hole. On the very last hole he saw
Palmer rifle a 7-iron to within five or six feet of the cup and
then sink that putt too to win the tournament.

No one who has not been in such a position can fully com-
prehend the elation of winning any golf tournament, let alone
one with so much prestige as the Masters. The money to be
eventually earned by such a feat is tremendous, of course, but
it takes second place to the deep and powerful satisfaction of
knowing that forever and ever you will always have that title
— Masters champion or U.S. Open champion or whatever —

after your name. It may be impossible for anyone not in golf to appreciate the nightmarish feeling that comes when something you know you have won is suddenly snatched away — for the second time. Visualize the man dying of thirst in the desert who dives headlong into a cool stream of water only to find that it is a mirage and you will be pretty close to knowing how Ken felt. He has said that his mental anguish over Palmer's last-minute victory was so great that it was days before he could really take in what had happened.

From then on Ken or Ken's game was never the same. In August he won the Milwaukee Open, but it was his last victory for the next three years at least. Ken's fast start permitted him to finish second on the money list with $41,230 to Palmer's $75,263, but the next year he slipped to fourteenth, winning $25,572, down to sixty-sixth in 1962 with a scant $6,951, and all the way to ninety-fourth in 1963 with $3,848. Little things began to go wrong. He hurt his back and he hurt his wrist. His mind didn't seem to be on what he was doing. He would sign an incorrectly marked scorecard and be disqualified. He would drive to the golf course, forget his parking sticker and be obliged to park a mile from the clubhouse and drag his bag all the way in on foot. In the Palm Springs Desert Classic, which is a pro-amateur tournament for the first four rounds, he hit the ball of one of his amateur partners by mistake and was disqualified for that. His tie-in as the playing professional at the Palo Alto Hills Golf and Country Club broke up over a disagreement about whether or not Ken was living up to his part of the contract or not.

The worst thing of all, though, was what happened to his once beautifully balanced swing. He started crouching over the ball like a sprinter at the starting blocks. His backswing was so fast all you could see of it was the big loop at the top.

On the downswing he cut across the ball from outside the the line to the target, instead of from squarely behind it as he had always done before. He thus was never able to hit the ball with the same old Venturi firmness. Even his putting stroke fell apart. In Ken's once confident hands a putter soon looked like a paperweight at the end of a long string.

A number of his friends tried to point out one or two of the more obvious flaws in his game, but Ken had made up his mind to work things out for himself. He wasn't about to take advice from anybody. Once I told him: "Ken, you're cutting across the ball all the time from the outside."

"That's the way I want to do it," he grumbled at me.

One of Ken's difficulties stemmed from his deep-seated self-assurance. When he first came out on the tour he was one of the best players around, even though he had just turned professional. He didn't doubt his ability or his destiny one bit and he didn't care if he told you about it either. Ken wasn't conceited in the usual sense of the word and he didn't brag, but cocky is too mild a description for the confidence he felt in himself. The result was that when he began to fall into bad habits, he felt too much pride to start listening when anyone tried to tell him what he might do to correct them.

People hear a lot about Palmer's fatigue and Nicklaus's sore hip or strained shoulder. They are on top and it is only natural that their aches and pains should be important news. But one thing few people hear from Venturi, except when he is forced to talk about them, are the physical ailments that have hurt his game: a back that pops out every now and then when he bends over to pick his ball out of the cup; a wrist that is constantly giving him pain and makes it hard for him to grip the club or swing it the way he would like to. All these have contributed to his collapse in the last few years.

But Ken's is a story of great courage because, despite the humiliation he must feel every time he misses the cut and has to pick up and move to the next stop while the rest of the players he once beat consistently remain to play, he continues to plug away with the determination of a terrier. I have come to have more admiration for Ken Venturi than almost anyone else on the tour. If he ever does come back and start winning again, and it just may happen fairly soon, it will be one of the great success stories of golf.

# 7 / *Two years in purgatory*

Mike Souchak and Ken Venturi were kings before they crashed and their slumps, therefore, have contained an element of tragedy that on the surface seems to be missing from the prolonged setbacks faced by lesser players. Even to less promising golfers, however, a slump can be a tough ordeal. The slimmer the bankroll to begin with the more critical the slump becomes. Pathetic Jack Belsey, the man who has missed a hundred cutoffs, has never been out of a slump. Palmer is considered to be on the skids if he goes a month without winning a tournament. But in one form or another every player on the tour goes through long periods of time when he seems to have lost his ability to play the kind of golf he is accustomed to playing. Look at my friend Tommy Jacobs, for instance. After he won the Denver Open in September of 1958 Tommy went through a dry spell of thirty-nine months before he won another tournament. In his rookie year of 1959 husky Mason Rudolph won the Golden Gate Open, held in San Francisco in September, and thus established himself as a golfer of exceptional promise. After this bright beginning he was still able to win good money, but it was forty-nine months before he won another golf tournament. I don't need to go on. Few players fade the way Souchak and Venturi have faded, but they all have to face the crisis of a slump eventually.

A good many of these form reversals are caused by bad putting, or what a player imagines to be bad putting. More probably it's just that he can't hit his iron shots close to the hole. Out here on the tour there is an incantation that is used by almost every player who is having trouble turning in respectable scores. "Why, I'm hitting the ball great from tee to green," he will say, "but I can't buy a putt."

It is true that many of us talk up our bad putting too much, and occasionally we start talking ourselves into really doing it. The feeling with just about every player on the tour is that he is a great striker of the ball; if he could only master that finicky little thing called the putting stroke he'd really show people how to play the game. Despite the exaggerations some players really do putt badly, a few at all times, others in frustrating patches. Most of us expect to hole at least one long putt — say of 40 to 60 feet — a round. We also expect an occasional three-putt green; also about one a round. But if we do not drop any long ones at all or stumble through an unreasonable amount of three-putt greens, then we begin to fret. We figure 32 putts for 18 holes is maximum. More than that and you are giving strokes they don't deserve to the rest of the field. If it happens a few times it begins to have a bad effect on the rest of your game. You force your approach shots to get them so close to the hole that you can't possibly miss the putt. The result is that you then start hitting bad shots because you are trying to get more out of yourself than is there.

What happened to my game in 1959 and 1960 was pretty terrifying to me at the time, but I have learned in my years on the tour that it is standard procedure. At the conclusion of my fine rookie year of 1958 I did not see any way I could fail to improve in 1959. I had won $16,000 in official and unofficial money (it's all official, in my opinion, when you go to spend it) and I intended to double that figure in the ensuing year. I had come very close to winning tournaments as a freshman. In my sophomore season I was not just going to come close, I was darn well going to win one. Even my sponsor, Crocker, was mightily impressed. He drew up a written contract and improved the terms. At least I thought he had improved the terms. My advance would now be $14,000 a year, and so I would not have to start sharing my earnings with him — two-thirds for me, one-third for him — until I had reached this higher level. With the financial problem at least temporarily out of the way I was free to concentrate on my golf.

As I mentioned earlier I realized that to really begin winning I had to produce shots with a high trajectory. This would not only improve my accuracy but help eliminate the bad bounces that often punish the low line drives. Golf has a tremendous element of chance. The whole idea of the game is to reduce chance as much as possible. Out on the tour a player won't get even close to the winner's circle if he doesn't learn to stick his iron shots close to the pin on hole after hole.

My idea about raising the trajectory of my shots was a very sound one, only I went about it in completely the wrong way. First of all, I figured that I must learn to fade the ball slightly from left to right. This would give me the necessary loft and soft flight to insure that the ball would stop quickly when it hit. So I altered my grip to bring this about. I turned my hands counterclockwise over the top of the club so that my left thumb rested along the top of the shaft and my right thumb along the left top. This is the kind of grip that sets up a left to right fade because it minimizes the power of the right hand, making it easier to keep the face of the club in an open position as it comes into the ball. In other words the face of the club will be ever so slightly turned to the right of the target at impact. This will impart a clockwise spin to the ball as it leaps off the clubhead, which in turn creates a left to right trajectory.

Another adjustment I made was to keep the ball back toward the center of my stance. The result of this maneuver was unfortunate. As I came down into the ball my hips and hands would get way ahead of it. I was hitting the ball with an open clubface, but I was also *starting* the shot off toward the right. Most of my shots headed right of the target and then faded even farther right. Under these circumstances I was lucky to stay on the golf course.

Today I know enough about the swing to realize what should be done. The ball must be played more off the left foot, out where the loft of the club can really get it into the air, and a strong effort made to stay down on each shot. This means keeping the right shoulder underneath the head as the club goes through the ball and moving the hands out toward the target for as long a distance as possible. It not only produces a higher trajectory, but also a good firm shot. Once a player has started to experiment with his game as I was doing, however, it becomes almost impossible to get back on an even keel. It's like trying to cut down and even up the legs of a wobbly table.

Another thing happened to me — or to part of me — at the tail end of 1958 that affected my play during 1959. No doubt it was more psychological than anything else, but it caused me a lot of grief. In December I went over to Sun Valley, where I had made quite a few friends in my days at Elko, for a short holiday. It was very cold and I had just come from a warm climate. I had my clubs with me and one day put on a sort of impromptu driving exhibition for a bunch of the ski instructors there. Sigi Engl was the head instructor and at that time was to ski instruction what Hogan was to golf. He and his staff were all avid golf nuts and they were watching with what I assumed was admiration as I stood on the first tee of the golf course in Sun Valley smashing drives toward the first green about 310 yards away. The driver I was using was absolutely my favorite club, one that I trusted like an old friend. This happens to a lot of players. Sam Snead has a driver he has been using for over twenty years. He just keeps repairing it. Dow Finsterwald owns a putter he has used for fourteen years. With drivers, putters, wedges, clubs we use all the time, it is quite normal to form an almost human attachment because they mean so much to our livelihood. That's the way I felt about this driver.

Eventually, I really uncorked a long one. It stopped right on the front edge of the green. When I bent over to pick the tee out of the ground and tee up another ball I took a close look at the clubhead. The wood had shattered completely right at the neck. I felt like a boy who has just seen his dog run over by a car. I almost cried. It was over a year before I got another that satisfied me.

The signs of my impending collapse were not visible when the 1959 winter tour opened in Los Angeles. I finished seventeenth in the tournament at which Ken Venturi beat out Art Wall by shooting a final-round 63. I bypassed Tijuana this time and went straight up to Pebble Beach to get ready for the Crosby. Unfortunately I wrenched a disc in my back and had to drop out after the first round. I was ready to play again when the circuit reached San Diego at the end of January. In those days the San Diego Open was played at the Mission Valley Country Club. The course has a creek or two ambling through it but for the most part you can just stand

up and rocket the ball in any direction and still have a relatively easy shot to the green. He who putts well will score
well. I putted well for two rounds and was in fifth place with
a 135, just two shots back of leader Mike Souchak. The
weather turned bad for the third round, so did my putting
and I shot myself out of contention for the lead with a 74.
The record book has me down for a 79 on the final day. That
looks pretty woeful, but considering what happened the night
before it was a pretty good round of golf.

An obvious necessity for players on the tour, notably the
bachelors, is women. We are out-of-doors all day, getting
plenty of exercise and fresh air, and physically at least all of
us are as healthy as forest rangers. Unlike the woods, however, there are always plenty of women around and a single
man has a hard time keeping his mind on his work.

I was staying at the Stardust Motel, right by the course,
and on the Saturday night before the final round of the '59
San Diego Open I received a phone call from this really
terrific-looking model I had met in San Diego the year before.
I invited her over for dinner. This was the beginning of a
long evening and we enjoyed every minute of it. I figured I
could play in a golf tournament every week, but it wasn't
every week I could have a heavy date with a girl who looked
like a Greek goddess. The next morning when I walked out
onto the first tee I was pretty relaxed and pretty tired. I didn't
care whether I shot 59, 79 or 199.

In my early years on the tour I think you could put several
of my bad rounds down to extracurricular activities at night.
I was not the only one, of course, but after a golfer has been
out on the circuit for a while he learns how to handle his
dating so that is doesn't interfere with his golf. The first rule
usually is no woman-chasing after Wednesday. If a man

hasn't gotten himself fixed up by the middle of the week it will take too many drinks and too many late hours to do so. By then the tournament is in progress and all energies should be devoted to it. On Saturday night, the eve of the final round, even the object of a heavy date should be sent home early. It is not too surprising that an excess of activity of this sort can have a debilitating effect on a golfer's play the next day.

All of these lessons take a while to learn. On the tour you can't live the way you do at home, of course, but you don't want to make the change too drastic. It isn't necessary, in fact, to do so. The main idea is to cut down on the late nights. If a player is accustomed to having a couple of cocktails before dinner he should go ahead and have a couple of cocktails before dinner. If he is used to enjoying the company of a woman two or three times a week, then he should go ahead and enjoy it. I have never denied myself a drink or a good dinner or a party while I am out on tour, provided I get enough rest. The most important thing to keep, in golf, is a good attitude and a clear mind. If a man gets jumpy because he is not doing the things he is accustomed to doing it will have a bad effect on his game.

I wish I could have put down all my bad rounds in 1959 to overindulgence. Unfortunately it was due more often to bad play and a bad temper. Relatively unknown players like Wes Ellis, Howie Johnson and Ernie Vossler were winning tournaments as the winter tour moved through the West and into Florida, but I was not coming close and it was beginning to build into a constant source of anxiety. Finally, at St. Petersburg, things reached something of a climax.

In the first round of the St. Petersburg Open, played at the Lakewood Country Club, just southwest of town, my putts began to drop as if the hole was a foot wide, not 4¼ inches.

I tied for first place at 66 with long-hitting George Bayer and an unknown pro named Tom Mahan, Jr. This was an exceptionally good score because Florida courses are difficult for a Californian like myself until he gets used to them. They are all as flat as a football field and the greens, to make each course at least mildly interesting, are built up on mounded plateaus. Missing a green means being faced with a tricky little pitch shot up a steep slope and often off a bare, sandy lie. It wasn't the type of shot I had learned to play.

My putting went back to normal on the second and third days and I shot a 76 each time. By the last round I simply didn't give a damn. I was paired with big Chick Harbert, a veteran player I had become pretty friendly with, and Walter Burkemo. I actually started to hit the ball pretty well. On the twelfth or thirteenth hole, I've forgotten exactly which one but I know it was a real tough par four that could only be reached with two long wood shots, my second shot was a beauty and stopped about 15 feet from the hole. My first putt ran about a foot and a half past the hole. Then I missed coming back. I was so enraged that I just reached out with my putter and began jabbing the ball back and forth as if I was playing polo. It finally popped in and I snarled to Chick, "Give me a 12 on the hole."

"No, goddamnit," he said with a laugh as we walked off the green. "You made it in 11, but I lost a lot of cash on you. I bet Walter here you'd get down in 10."

Chick was trying to pass the incident off with a little humor but I didn't think it was particularly funny. Neither, really, did Chick. He gave me a short lecture on the way to the next tee.

"Look," he said, "if you're not going to try then don't bother to come out here and drive yourself crazy. Some days you are just going to have to work very hard to shoot a 74 or 75. If you're not willing to put up with it then you're in the wrong business."

This was excellent advice. When a rookie comes out on the tour he is all fired up and his interest is sky-high. After a long period of good playing he may suddenly start running into difficulties. Often he thinks that maybe he isn't scoring well because his game has gone bad. This is not always the reason, but often the newcomer will get discouraged and quit trying hard. The result is a total letdown. Ken Venturi who, until Jack Nicklaus came out on the tour, had had the best rookie year of any pro in history, gave me some words of advice to counteract this kind of emotional letdown.

"Play as hard as you can," Ken has always told me, "so that when you walk off the course with a 75 or 76 you can honestly say to yourself that that was absolutely the best score you could turn in that day. Not every day can you shoot a 66 or a 67."

I could have thought back to that first little tournament I had won, the Imperial Valley Open, for an excellent example of how this philosophy works. In the Imperial Valley event I had played badly the first few holes of the final round, but I had kept plugging away and stayed close to par. When finally the birdies began to fall I was in a position to take full advantage of them and eventually won the tournament. This was advice that yielded dividends in 1962 and '63 when I finally began to heed it in earnest, but back in the gloomy years of 1959 and '60 it simply did not register. The next week after St. Pete, at the Azalea Open, I shot 79–75–80–79, for a 313. It was just about the worst score I had ever produced in a 72-hole golf tournament. From then on, until the fall when I made a run at winning in Portland, Oregon, I never even came close. At the Gleneagles Open in Chicago in June I missed a 36-hole cutoff for the first time. Then stretched the string to four in a row by missing the cut at three more tournaments — the rich Buick Open, in Flint, the prestigious Western Open in Pittsburg, and the Insurance City Open in Hartford. In several tournaments I would shoot one, two, or even three good rounds, but always seemed to have one really bad day that wiped out everything else.

The Portland Open, played the first week in October, supplies a neat anatomy of how a player can blow a tournament even when he has his nerves under control. I started out with a 65 and was leading by two shots over Jim Ferree and Jay Hebert. My second-round 68 slipped me back into a tie for first with Bill Casper and a third-round 69 left me all alone in second, but only two shots back of Casper. We were playing at the Portland Golf Club, a fairly short and easy course, and since I was playing well, I thought I had an excellent chance to win.

On the very first hole my drive landed on the left side of the fairway and then kicked left smack under a tree. A bad break. I had to chip the ball back onto the fairway and made a bogey. On the second hole I thought to myself, "I must get that lost stroke back immediately." I hit a fine shot 15 feet from the cup, but charged the putt so hard in my eagerness to make the birdie that the ball skidded several feet past and I missed coming back. Rather quickly, I found myself two over par while the other contenders were dipping one or two shots under par. The third hole required nothing but a drive and a short wedge shot, but the cup had been cut into the back edge of the green. I hit my wedge approach too boldly, the ball hit deep into the green and then rolled down over the back side. I tried frantically to chip the ball right into the hole with a 7-iron, but ran it far past instead and two-putted for my third straight bogey. By that time I was a pocketful of strokes out of contention for the tournament title, and so I decided right then and there just to try to win a good-sized check. Stop this charging for birdies baloney, I told myself, and play sensible golf. What happened? I played the last 15 holes two under par and got back into a tie for fifth place, earning $1000. Why had I blown such a good chance to win? Well, first of all, Casper shot a 69, but that wasn't anything I couldn't have beaten on this fairly easy golf course. Nerves? No. I felt fine going into the final round, even confident. The flaw lay in my attitude. If it had been a good one I could have gone ahead after the bad break on the first hole, played a normal game of golf and gotten my share of birdies. But I became angry and greedy. I was going to grab those birdies as soon as possible rather than just wait for them to come. The result after three holes? Three over par, instead of even par or possibly one under, and completely out of the tournament.

The dismal year of 1959 ended at Coral Cables, Florida, and I went on home to Oakland. After the fine start I had made on the tour in 1958 the season just ended had naturally been an unpleasant experience. I had lost a lot of confidence in myself and my game. Emotionally, I swung from one extreme to the other. If I wasn't going to play well, I began to think, "Oh the hell with it," and I would blow sky-high, even shooting rounds in the 80's. But, I thought, other players have had bad years and then have come back. I imagined that 1959 was just such a year. As it turned out the disappointments of 1959 were merely an overture to the sad, sad blues I was singing all during 1960.

I should have guessed before the new year started that it

was going to be a bad one. I was unlucky from the very beginning. During the Christmas holidays I went skiing in Sun Valley, where I had busted my driver the year before, took a bad spill and cracked a couple of ribs. That put me out of the Los Angeles Open. The following week in the Yorba Linda Open I shot my good round the first day, a course-record 66, and led the tournament. Then finished 75, 74, 73, to tie for twenty-fifth. The next week, at San Diego, I won the pro-am before the start of the tournament with a 67 and then went on to miss the cut. This exasperating kind of thing happened a lot to me that year — and in fact it does happen to many seasoned players — but with me it was an indication of my continued lousy mental attitude. I'd play the pro-am one way and the tournament another. In the pro-am I'd be loose and relaxed, little bad breaks wouldn't bother me. In the tournament I'd get all tightened up and if anything went even slightly wrong I'd blow up. The result was that my scores went up and down like an elevator, but mostly they were up. I missed the cut just about as often as I made it and pretty soon the only cut I really wanted to make was in the vicinity of my neck and with a nice sharp razor. I was mad and miserable from the moment I got up in the morning until the moment I went to bed. Nothing was going right. I wasn't sleeping well, I wasn't eating well. I was living it up a lot, at least in the sense of getting half gassed all the time and chasing after women, but this was a false, very insecure way of trying to keep myself at some sort of even pitch. I could understand for the first time what it meant and how it could happen that people had nervous breakdowns. I was trying desperately hard to do something — play winning golf — without any result. In fact my efforts were carrying me speedily in the opposite direction. I'd completely lost all sense of values; off the golf course, on the golf course. Everything looked tough to me. A wide-open little pitch shot looked tough. A two-foot putt looked tough. I wondered if I could get it down. There was no such thing as *knowing* I could do anything. It was always "I can't do it." Or at least a real negative, "What if I don't do it." If I'd make a good shot or sink a putt I'd think, "Well, I was lucky." Three times I was fined for throwing clubs. I got up in the morning to shave and hated the sight of my face in the mirror. I hated golf and was ashamed to be a professional golfer. Finally the other players began to talk to me. Venturi, Chick Harbert, Don January, all took me aside and tried to calm me down, straighten me out. I was having none of it. This was an extreme case, but it was what practically every player begins to go through when he hits a prolonged slump. What keeps him playing? Usually two things: the hope that the slump will suddenly end, and the fact that he usually doesn't know anything but golf.

Finally one evening in St. Paul things had gotten so bad that Dow Finsterwald asked me to come by his room for a fight talk. No player on the tour likes to take another aside and lecture him on his behavior, so it is easy to guess what bad shape I was in. I dropped by his room at the St. Paul Hotel, he poured me out a scotch and then laid it on the line.

"Look," he said. "Don't you think you could give it a better try out here if you got hold of yourself, all the way down the line?" Cut out the nonsensical drinking, he said. You can't belt down half a bottle of scotch at night and expect to play halfway decently the next day. Don't go out on the golf course all p.o.'d at the world. You can't play well then, either. Develop a more cheerful and hopeful mental attitude or you will never be able to play well again.

Some of these talks began to seep through. I guess I was lucky that people cared enough about me to deliver them. I had never tried to do anything underhanded to anyone else out on the tour. I just liked to have a good time, to play around, have a few laughs, tell a few jokes, buy everyone a drink or let them buy me one. I even tried to pass the girls around or find out for everyone where the good ones were in that particular town. It was inevitable that Pott, Jacobs and Ferree began to drift out of my immediate circle altogether. Jacobs and Pott both had gotten married in 1959 and John finally won his first golf tournament in 1960. It was the Dallas Open, played the first week in September, and ironically enough I missed the cut that week.

Just before my last tournament of the year I got a rather inspiring capsule definition of a winning attitude from Arnold Palmer. You might say that it differed somewhat from my own. This was the year, of course, that Palmer had beaten Venturi in the Masters, finishing birdie-birdie. He had also won the Palm Springs Desert Classic with a 66 and a 65 over the last two rounds and the U.S. Open with a final-round 65. In addition, he had won at the Texas Open, at Baton Rouge and at Pensacola. Now in November he had won the Mobile Open with a final-round 65. The dazzling Palmer finish was becoming part of golf history.

After the Mobile tournament Palmer and I were picked up by some mutual friends of ours and flown down to New Orleans in their Twin Cessna. We spent the night with them in New Orleans, went to a cocktail party the following afternoon and spent our last night, prior to flying over to West Palm Beach for the tournament there, on our host's yacht. Palmer and I were bunked together on a double-decker and I had trouble getting to sleep. The lights had been out for about half an hour when I called down and asked Arnold if he were asleep. He wasn't so we talked and smoked for a while before finally dropping off. At one point I just had to ask him a question that had been bothering every player on the tour.

"Do you realize what you have really done this year?" I said.

"What do you mean, 'what I've really done'?" he asked.

"Well, winning what you have the way you have," I said. "Finishing birdie-birdie to win the Masters. Shooting a 65 on the last round to win the Open. It seems so fantastic, so superhuman to have done these things in that way." His answer supplied, I think, the clue as to why so many successful athletes are that way.

"I've never thought of it in those terms," he said. "I just kind of see what it is I have to do, and I just make up my mind that I'm going to do it. If I have a long putt to make I just think about making that putt. I shut from my mind the thought of missing it or all the other stuff that would come from my missing it."

With this positive philosophy fresh in my mind I finished out the year in grand style. At West Palm Beach I tied for first in the pro-am with a 67 and then missed the cut. In the last tournament of the year, at Coral Gables, I won the pro-am with a 65 and finished the tournament out of the money. Then I flew home. During the trip I began to go over the year just past. I realized that in just about every tournament I had had one good round, a very good round. There was therefore something there that at least gave me the idea that, doggonit, somewhere, somehow, by some sort of means, I could make a success of professional golf. Getting to the end of 1960 had been getting to the end of the high wire during a circus act. That alone had taken something. I was beginning to believe at last that golf involved something more than just hitting a golf ball. The year just past had been one of self-persecution. If I started off with a good round, would I give myself the benefit of the doubt and imagine that I had been doing something well? No sir. I'd go out that night and party it up because I had told myself that I couldn't do it again, that I was going to go out and goof it up some way or other. Very few people know the mental hell a player on the tour can go through. But I thought I would give the tour just one more year, that was all. I thought, I've suffered enough with this goddamn game. I'm going out there one more time and put myself through that ordeal just one more time. Then I will quit for good. I will have given it a fling whether I give my best or not. I'll have tried it. I don't want that kind of life. To sit looking at the four walls of my motel room, nothing to do for the next three days until I can try to qualify for the next tournament, worrying about shooting 78 or 79 and being embarrassed to have my scores put up on the scoreboard with those of the other players, with those of my close friends. I had had it. I'd played the act. I had played the bit as a playboy. I was even getting tired of that. You can only drink so many bottles of Scotch and go to so many nightclubs. There isn't any excitement in that after a while. I could see how wealthy people went off their rockers too. I was fed up with the luxury hotel rooms, the luxury resorts, and the luxury restaurants. It was totally boring. It was a terrifying ordeal to get up in the morning and go out on the golf course. I could hardly wait until I was back off the course. I had lost two things. I had lost determination and I had lost my desire to play the game. I had reached the point where I hated to look at a golf club or a golf ball or a golf course.

Even my sponsor, to whom I now owed about $10,000, wanted me to quit. Crocker had called me two or three times during the year explaining that he would wipe off the debt if only I would give up tournament golf. I had made up my mind, however. One more year. When I went home to the family the pressures began to ease off. I began to live like a normal human being again. Eight hours' sleep every night. Seeing my old friends, going out to dinner with them and not talking about golf. Taking out girls who didn't know anything about golf. When the tour started again I was going to try to change my attitude and control my temper. I didn't look forward to doing it and I didn't look forward to having any success doing it, but I was still young and I was going to give it one more year of my youth. My new resolutions began to have their effect. It was just about this time that things began to take a turn for the better. I went south for a five-week tournament tour of the Caribbean and certain events conspired to convince me that I really could be a pretty good golfer after all.

# 8 / *Caribbean tour*

THE five week offshoot of the regular tour, called the Caribbean circuit, was something I first heard about from my
traveling companions Pott, Jacobs and Ferree. Swinging
down through Panama, Venezuela, Puerto Rico and now
Colombia it is to the tournament program in the States what
a trunk line is to a railroad. It curls away from the United
States in February while the regular tour is in California. It
picks it up again in March at Florida. About fifty golfers,
forty teaching and ten touring pros, take the full swing and
my buddies had all made it at least once prior to 1961. For
them it had been a chance to break the routine of the tour in
the States, get away from everything, be in contention in a
tournament every week and also come out of the trip with a
tidy little profit. In the winter of 1961 I had blasted off onto
another indifferent year, and when the Caribbean tournament
committee offered me a last-minute invitation (Bob Toski had
involved himself in a new golf course deal and had pulled
out.) I jumped at the chance. The invitation was extended
while I was playing in the Palm Springs Classic. As soon as
that tournament was over I flew home to Oakland to pack and
then flew back to Los Angeles in time to catch the plane that
was taking the handful of players who came straight off the
U.S. tour.

Including myself there were six regular touring pros on the

plane — tough little Billy Maxwell, who had won the Palm Springs Classic when Ken Venturi had blown it on the fifteenth hole by hitting two shots out of bounds, Ernie Vossler, a Texan who was making his third trip south, Don Whitt, a slender Californian who was to be my roommate on the tour and like myself was making it for the first time, my old friend Jim Ferree, and bubbly Dow Finsterwald, who was flying down just for the first tournament, the Panama Open. Also on the plane were several club pros who had been out on the coast playing the tour for a couple of months because their clubs back home were closed by snow. Unlike the rest of us these players were paying their own expenses all the way. Down in the Caribbean they are called Rabbits. It's a name that bobs up on the U.S. tour from time to time and I've never been able to pin down its derivation. Maybe a player is called a rabbit when he only gets a nibble of prize money from time to time and never gets a big bite of the lettuce.

The so-called name pros were being sponsored. In other words all our expenses for food, lodging, transportation, etc., were taken care of by various sponsors in each city. We also received a guarantee against prize money of $200 a week. Since each tournament paid a total purse of $10,000 there existed an excellent chance for the standout golfers to improve considerably on the guarantee. I was not too sure that I fitted into that category, but it was comforting to know that as a sponsored player anything I made would be pure gravy.

As I flopped back in my seat for the long seven-hour trip from Los Angeles to Panama City, I was feeling pretty good about this Caribbean tour. I figured that for the first time in longer than I cared to recall I would be in contention every week. In addition, there is no 36-hole cutoff in the Caribbean so I knew that however badly I played I would be able to

I had just rolled in a 25-foot birdie putt on the last hole to lead the 1963 Masters and felt pretty delirious until . . .

Jack Nicklaus, from almost right out of the teeth of the mammoth crowd, hit this second shot onto the same green.

Johnny Pott (upper left), Tommy Jacobs (upper right, with wife Sally) and Jim Ferree (below), doffing his cock-eyed straw hat after holing the putt that won the 1958 Vancouver Open, were the close and indispensable friends of my rookie year.

Hitting each shot with almost arrogant confidence, slender Ken Venturi (above) and muscular Mike Souchak (below) reached their peaks during 1960; then their careers took a strange turn.

*John Zimmerman – Sports Illustrated*     *John Zimmerman – Sports Illustrated*

The 1960 U.S. Open in Denver provided this sharp contrast between victorious Arnold Palmer, flinging his cap skyward after holing the winning putt, and disconsolate Mike Souchak, burying his face in a damp towel on the sixty-fifth tee as his hopes sank.

Two of golf's great showmen in action. Phil Rodgers (left) skips across the green after sinking a putt in the 1963 Los Angeles Open, and Gary Player (below) brandishes a joyous fist after holing a long putt in the 1963 Masters.

*James Drake — Sports Illustrated*

*Bath — Sports Illustrated*

*Richard Meek – Sports Illustra*

This is the perilous view from the eighteenth tee at the Augusta National, home of the Masters tournament. The hole is 420 yards long, uphill most of the way, and bends sharply around the trees at the right to a three-level green.

The tension of big-time golf is etched in the faces of Arnold Palmer, hitting, and Julius Boros, watching, as they play off their tie with Jacky Cupit at the 1963 U.S. Open in Brookline, Massachusetts.

During a restful vacation from the hectic life of the tour, Betty and I
enjoy champagne and dinner at the Blue Fox restaurant in San Francisco.

stick it out for the full 72 holes. I was also tremendously en-
couraged by the fact that I would have a real chance to practice each day. I could work hard and thoroughly on putting
some zip into my game because the field at each tournament
would be small and the practice area would be uncrowded.
This is quite a contrast with the situation that prevails on the
winter tour in the States. At home, not only is the weather
often very bad, but there are so many players competing during the winter months that the practice tee begins to look
like a movie mob scene. A player is lucky to get himself a
square yard of badly torn up turf.

From the Panama City airport we were driven into the El
Panama Hilton Hotel, which sat on the northern edge of the
city almost smack against the jungle that surrounds it. It was
a very large, modern, comfortable and pleasant building. Out
back were a spacious dining patio, a swimming pool and
cabana type swimming lockers. It also had a view of the
Pacific Ocean, about two miles to the south.

The golf course was also pretty exciting — if that is the
word. The clubhouse sat high on the top of a hill and was
open to the breeze on all four sides. This created a cooling
crossdraft in the hot weather. The rainy season had ended a
few weeks earlier and the course was baked out like a tortilla.
Wide cracks had appeared in the dry red soil of the fairways,
and to make playing conditions as close as possible to normal
white stakes were driven along the sides of all fairways, right
up to the very edge of the greens. If a player hit the ball so
that it remained within these white stakes it meant that he
could roll it around on the sparse grass of the fairway with his
clubhead until he obtained a lie that satisfied him. Anyone
who knocked his ball outside the rows of stakes just dropped
to his knees and prayed. It would quite probably wind up in

a crack, among rocks, or at best on a stretch of hard, smooth clay. Obviously, it was important to keep the ball on the fairway. These conditions reminded me of something Tommy Jacobs had warned me to expect when the tour hit the Caymanas golf course in Jamaica, a stop that is no longer on the schedule. There was so much jagged rock and coral adjacent to the fairways there, he said, than anyone unfortunate enough to hit a shot off line was smart not to find the ball at all. It was far better to declare the ball lost, take the two-shot penalty called for in this case and play another ball, than to find the first one and take possibly several ineffectual slashes trying to get it back in play.

I found that the Panama City golf course was also pretty difficult to get used to, and finished twenty-third place with a 295 for 72 holes. I figured that was about par for that stage of the tour and so I wasn't too unhappy. I practiced both before and after each round, and found myself able to eliminate some of the hitting problems that had been plaguing me for two years. Besides, I was having a pretty good time in Panama City.

The fact that Don Whitt was my roommate for the two trips I made to the Caribbean was what made it possible for me to enjoy the tour so much. Don is a fine golfer who had not had much luck on the tour in the States since he won the Memphis and Kentucky Derby Opens back-to-back in the spring of 1959. He was a wonderful roommate, one of the rare people who takes his golfing very seriously when he is on the course, but can forget about it completely when he gets back to the hotel. Off the course we didn't spend much time worrying about the art of hitting a golf ball. Our routine during the week we stayed in Panama City — and it worked for both years we were there — was pretty unvaried. On the Caribbean tour you never have to tee off until late in the morning or early in the afternoon. We would get up around 8 or 9 o'clock, it was difficult to sleep later than that anyway in the hot climate, grab a quick breakfast and head downtown to shop. Panama City is a free port and you could buy a certain perfume for about $15, compared to $48 in the States or a $1000 Swiss watch for something like $300. One thing we learned was never to pay the first price asked, even in the big department stores. Panamanian storekeepers can spot a tourist just as quickly as any storekeeper in the world, and will immediately jack up the list price for the visitor's benefit.

Then, Don and I would come back to lie by the pool and enrich our tans, take a light lunch, and head out to the golf course, about a thirty minute ride by cab. We'd play our golf, come back to the hotel and drink some of the liquor that the Seagram Distillers, which cosponsors the tour, left in every player's room at each stop. Or we'd go down to the bar and swallow a few frozen daiquiris, our favorite meal in the torrid Caribbean. We'd have dinner, try to scout up a decent night-club (there aren't many in Panama City), and then head for bed around 12 or 1 o'clock. Believe me, it was a pleasant vacation from the demanding grind of the tour in the U.S.

One night we had dinner in the home of the Panama Open tournament director, a rugged, pleasant American named Dick Dehlinger who had come down to Panama from Buffalo back in 1940. He had worked as a Canal policeman, ship cargo inspector on the docks, gone into the auto financing business and is now prospering in the real estate, construction and trading stamp business. The small group of people he had at his home that night included some of the players from the tournament as well as the former president of Panama, Ricardo Arias.

A few nights later, the tournament was over, and after a few frozen daiquiris I had stumbled into bed quite early. But the pre-Lent carnival was on and the music was so loud that I couldn't sleep, finally got up, dressed and went downstairs. A huge crowd had formed on the dance floor and had moved back to clear an area in the center of the floor. There was the beautiful dark-haired, dark-eyed Carnival Queen and she looked dazzling in her white gown and golden crown. She was doing a lively cha-cha with her partner and they looked as capable as the best professional dance teams I had ever seen back in the States. Then I got a closer look at her partner. It was nobody but my good old roomie, Don Whitt. The next moment I could hardly believe my eyes as he hopped up onto the bandstand and began leading the orchestra, shaking a couple of maracas. He was completely engrossed in his merrymaking and even looked Latin with his slim build, his deep tan and short, but dark sideburns. Don is such a terrific dancer and mingler with people that if it was ever left to me to pick a golfer to make a goodwill tour abroad he would be one of my first choices. In Panama they were ready to make him King of the Carnival.

Sleepless and groggy the troop of golfers made the four-hour trip to Maracaibo, Venezuela, early the next afternoon. It was just as well we were in something of a daze because a first look at Maracaibo is enough to put anyone in a state of shock. It is a hot, flat, dusty, wind-wracked oil town on the shores of gigantic Lake Maracaibo. The lake looks absolutely cool and beautiful, but this just seemed to increase our discomfort from the unchanging heat. The lake's surface was covered with a thin oil slick and was as brown as mud. The town is a big one, with a population of 400,000 and is built primarily of square, brightly colored little houses. The golf course was situated in a vast desert of red clay and cactus about fifteen miles outside of town. This section of the country looks like West Texas at the worst time of the year, and on the way to the golf course we had to drive through slums where thousands of people lived in lines of little tin shacks that must have been like ovens during the boiling hot days and nights.

The golf course, considering its setting, was magnificent. Green fairways and huge, elevated and lush green putting surfaces. The club had to pour a million and a half gallons of water a day on the course or it would have died in a week. This helped contribute to a monthly maintenance bill of $18,000. We were all afraid to hit the ball off the fairway, however, so desolate was the wind swept, iguana-ridden land around the course.

The hotel we stayed at, the Del Lago, was a modern and comfortable one, though it was was deserted when we arrived on a Monday night. As we entered the lobby we could see and hear a dance quartet hammering away eerily on a tango in an empty cocktail lounge immediately adjacent to the lobby. During the day the hotel and its grounds were ideal. You couldn't swim in it, but the wide, palm-fringed lake was a cooling and restful sight at which to sit and gaze. It helped if there was a frozen daiquiri at hand.

The long, 7000-yard golf course and the high winds made the tournament a tough and exciting one. Don, who was as calm as a Venezuelan during siesta, played almost perfect golf and won the tournament with a 283. Roberto de Vicenzo, the large bearish Argentinian, made a strong challenge, but missed a four-foot putt on the next to last hole and finished second by a stroke. I thought I might even have a chance to win, but I tried to win it on the first couple of holes, three-putted them and shot a closing 79 which tied me for tenth place at 294 with Jim Ferree. Until then, however, I had played pretty well.

I'll never forget the caddy I had my first year in Maracaibo. He looked no more than four feet tall and was about fifty years old. He was barefooted, wore a pair of oversized coveralls rolled up to his knees and had about three teeth in his mouth. My golf bag was about as big and heavy as he was. He was cheerful, always laughing at everything, and as strong as a bull. When I hit the ball he'd grab the bag and set off after it like a cat after a chickadee, his straw hat barely sticking to his head as he scuttled down the fairway. The caddy fees down there were about two dollars a day, and at the end of the week I gave him his regular fee plus a $10 tip. He couldn't believe it, and showed the $10 bill to everyone who would look at it. I was delighted that so little could mean so much.

As our stay in Maracaibo drew to a close we looked forward eagerly to the next stop on the tour, Caracas. We had heard the city was beautiful and — since it is located at an elevation of 3500 feet — the climate cool. Weather-wise the climate was cool all right, but politically it turned out to be pretty hot. A couple of days before we left Maracaibo word passed rapidly through the players on the tour that the manager of the Tamanaco Hotel in Caracas, where we would stay, had received an anonymous threat that the hotel would be blown up. This seemed a little farfetched to most of us, but at least one golfer, young Dick Chase of Pittsburgh, decided he had had enough of the Caribbean tour. Despite the fact that his friends Mike Krak and Art Doering tried hard to dissuade him, he packed up and headed for the winter tour in the States. Maybe it was because of the bomb threat. Maybe it was because he'd shot

79 and 80 during the first two rounds of the Maracaibo tournament.

The government of Venezuela had only recently undergone the change from dictatorship to a democracy and there was still a great deal of unrest there and a strong anti-American sentiment. Vice President Nixon's riot-marred visit of 1958 was still fresh in our minds and most of us were pretty determined to stick close to the hotel, especially at night. We were quite content to confine the excitement to the golf course. Even the morning of our arrival what Caraquenians refer to as a *golpe*, or blow, took place. A small group of anti-government army officers had broken into the broadcasting studios of Radio Caracas and announced that the government had been overthrown. Government forces finally drove them out and then had to spend the rest of the day assuring Radio Caracas listeners that the government was still in business.

While Caracas may have been a very restless city it was also a very beautiful one. The first day a group of us — Whitt, myself, and three teaching pros, Stan Dudas, Stan Mosel and Sam Penecale, all from the New Jersey–Pennsylvania area — couldn't bear the thought of going to the course. We took the cable car up the side of the Venezuelean Alps on the north border of the city, to the cylindrically shaped Humbolt Hotel, which is not always full because it is quite expensive and not exactly accessible. We had the place practically to ourselves. We drank at the bar, went up to the darkened, deserted penthouse bar which looked out on a spectacular view, not only of the Caribbean 8000 feet below to the north but also of the city, glittering like a scale model 4500 feet below us to the south.

The week in Caracas was a glorious one. The skies were clear, the temperature a balmy 75 degrees and most of us hated to leave. Don won the tournament on a course that was in sharp contrast to the one we had played on the week before. It was only about 6200 yards long, but it was perched on a hilly slope directly above the city and was as narrow and winding as a mountain road. Don shot a 272 and won the tournament by eight shots, but I also had my moment of glory.

The Valle Arriba Country Club, where the tournament is played each year, is not exactly suited to a free-swinger like myself. In fact it is possible to knock the ball out of bounds on 17 holes. During the third round, however, I had played my best golf of the entire Caribbean trip and was six strokes under par after 15 holes. I had a great chance to break the course record of 65 that De Vicenzo had set in the first round simply by parring the last three holes. That didn't satisfy me, however; I was out to shoot 60.

On the sixteenth hole, a narrow par four of 390 yards, I hooked a 4-wood off the tee and the ball was just barely saved from rolling out-of-bounds by a clump of deep grass. I parred the hole. On the seventeenth, a par four of only 270 yards that runs along the bottom of a canyon, I hooked a 4-wood again, but it stayed in bounds by rolling down the slope alongside the canyon. It was in deep grass, however, and I had to scrape to make a bogey. On the eighteenth hole again I tore into my tee shot and hit it clear across the fairway. When I got to the ball it was only two feet in bounds. I parred the hole, but what turned out to be a 65 might just as easily have been six shots higher if God hadn't been looking out for me.

The night the tournament ended a festive dance was held at the club. A band called Billo's Caracas Boys whipped out a lively collection of Latin and American dance tunes and during an intermission the players were awarded their checks. This was more like the Harvest Moon prom in high school than the pro golf tour. I spent most of the night on the dance floor entwined with a lovely young girl who had dark hair, and the dark, hypnotic, sultry eyes that many Latin-American women possess. She was at least eighteen, very gay, very sweet, hardly spoke a word of English, but certainly must have put me under some sort of spell. After the dance, with me footing the bills, the girl, myself and her aunt the chaperone went nightclubbing and I didn't get to bed until dawn. The girl had a good time, but Caracas has the highest cost of living or playing of any city in the world. It was a long night for my wallet and the girl's aunt.

The tournament had ended on a Saturday because Sunday, February 28, 1961, was national census day in Venezuela. The government must have wanted to complete the census in record time because all of Venezuela had to place itself under what amounted to house arrest from 8 o'clock in the morning until 6 o'clock at night. This meant that hotel residents had to remain in their hotel, but fortunately the Tamanaco Hotel is the next best thing to a country club. It is located on a gentle mountain slope overlooking from the south the entire valley in which the city of Caracas nestles. On hand are a large swimming pool, bars, nightclubs, and even a nine-hole pitch and putt golf course. Its cosmopolitan atmosphere is testified to by the fact that at the newstand in the spacious lobby one can buy copies of the *New York Times*, the *New York Herald Tribune*, the *Wall Street Journal*, a daily called *Die Welt*, printed in Hamburg, Germany, the *London Daily Telegraph* and even baseball's weekly bible, the *Sporting News*.

On census Sunday the hotel manager, perhaps to keep the golfers out of trouble and give the rest of his guests a few laughs, sponsored a tournament on the pitch and putt course

and called it the Tamanaco Open. He should have called it
the Hangover Open. First prize was four days' free rent at
the hotel. Sponsored players got the equivalent in cash, about
$80. Don and I had needed a couple of daiquiris to stage a
recovery from the celebrating we did the night before and
were not at our competitive best. Bob Watson, a tall Texan
who had a club job in the New York City area, won the tournament with an eight under par 46. This victory over a bunch
of groggy players, who stumbled around in their bathing suits,
like owls in a bright sun didn't exactly qualify Watson for
the Masters, but he said that at least it gave him something
more than a good tan to show for five weeks in the Caribbean.

After this inspired pitch and putt tournament a crowd of
us went back up to the pool or played just slightly raucous
games of ping-pong and volley ball. Caleb Haye, a cheerful
young Jamaican who had been making the tour, brought his
pitching wedge up to the pool and I jumped in with it to
demonstrate the art of blasting a golf ball out of a foot of
water. Several others also tried but we succeeded in doing
nothing but soaking ourselves and everybody around the pool.
Finally Ernie Vossler, still wearing his shirt and his steel-
rimmed glasses, climbed in and thrashed away futilely for
five minutes.

"There's no way you can get this ball out of here," he kept
shouting in a Texas accent, but he kept laughing and shouting and thrashing at the water just the same. Heaven help
the hotel that has fifty professional golfers trapped in it for
a day.

Don Whitt finally put himself out of action by attempting
a somersault off the high diving board. A good diver ordinarily, Whitt, no doubt due to the effect of a daiquiri or
two, twisted his back so badly that he was barely able to

swing a club the following week at the Puerto Rico Open.

For a while it looked like we might never get to Puerto Rico at all. Many of the airlines were on strike and our Pan American flight was canceled. Caribbean tour supervisor George Hall, who was also the treasurer of the PGA, got on the phone and lined up a charter plane for all fifty of us. Don and I barely made it. We were both so exhausted that we overslept, missed the bus that carried the players out to the airport, and had to grab a cab for the hour-long trip. Then we sat around smoldering in the baking heat of the airport for two hours until the plane, a four-engine Viscount, was ready for the four-hour flight to San Juan. I, for one, was sorry to leave. Caracas had been a beautiful city and the people I had met there delightful. How different from the cheerless hustle and bustle of the States. Down here I was one of the top players and the people we met at each stop were extra nice on that account. As far as hospitality was concerned I didn't have to compete with the likes of Arnold Palmer or Sam Snead. The dozen sponsored players were the top dogs and the people who like to associate with the top dogs were stuck with us. I liked the people, I liked the city and I liked the girl I had taken out so much that I was determined to hurry back after our troupe had made its Puerto Rican appearance. By the time we got through at Puerto Rico, however, I was too tired even to think how I could have contemplated such an escapade.

We came down at San Juan airport late in the afternoon and I thought there would be a fight even before we got away from it. A swarm of photographers was on hand. Most of us were pretty tired and didn't feel much like posing, but we never had a chance to refuse. Someone grabbed Billy Maxwell, pulled his jacket down over his arms to form a very effective straightjacket, and the next day Billy was immortalized on the back page of the *San Juan Star,* the city's English-language paper. He looked like a baggy-pants comedian mugging for a sluggish nightclub audience. The picture had been cropped to include only Billy's face. His eyes were popping out of his head and his mouth was pursed up as if he was about to spit bullets.

About this time on the Caribbean tour everybody's temper was getting pretty frayed. We had been banging around hot climates trying vainly to understand foreign customs and a foreign language for three weeks and it was pretty hard on the nervous system. San Juan didn't make things any better nor did the golf course we played on there. A Miami Beach resident would think he had never left home. Big hotels, lots of tourists, too much traffic. The golf course at the Berwind Country Club is what a polite golfer would describe as a "sporty little lay-out," meaning, "My God, what a cow pasture!" It is crisscrossed by ditches and hopping all over it are the biggest toads I ever saw in my life, as big as pigeons. Sometimes they hop out of their holes just as you are about to hit a shot. You are so scared its all you can do to keep from dropping the club and sprinting back to the clubhouse. Well, what with the golf course, the toads, the heat and the ditches it was a tough tournament just to play in, let alone play well. Don and I were out of it from the beginning. Diver Don because of his strained back and I because of a sprained disposition. We only had one good bed in our room — at a hotel that was modern, but had a lobby so windy you practically had to crawl across it on hands and knees to reach the elevator — and the man who shot the low round of the day got it each night. The loser slept on a fold-out couch. I got the good bed the first night of the tournament by shooting a 72 to Don's 73, but he won it back on the second day with a 74 to my 75. I finished with a 69 and a 74 to hold the good bed for the rest of the week, but it was not much of a satisfaction. I seemed to be spending more time in Berwind's ditches than I did in the bed.

The only way to keep from hitting into one ditch after another was to deliberately play short of them, especially off the tee. This meant leaving the driver in the bag and hitting off the tee with an iron or a 3-wood. The fairways were so hard and dry, however, that even laying up in this manner didn't always work. On six holes my lay-up shots scuttled along the ground like motor scooters and vanished into one of the omnipresent crevices.

On the eighteenth it happened again. I played a perfect 3-wood off the tee and then watched it disappear. By the time I got down to the ditch I was ready to go off like a Roman candle. I took my 3-wood and hurled it down into the ditch on top of the ball.

Then I took my bag of clubs from the caddy and dropped it down on top of the ball and the 3-wood.

Then I turned to see what my caddy thought of *that,* but his face had turned white and he was backing off across the fairway. "*No, señor, no, señor,*" he begged. "*Por favor, por favor.*"

I was feeling in this mood right through the entire Puerto Rican visit. The frame of mind I had carried with me from the U.S. tour recurred and I was more than a little fed up with being a professional golfer. On the eve of the tournament Don and I ran into a friend from the States and the three of us went over to the Caribe Hilton for dinner. While waiting for our table we started talking with two girls who had come down from New Jersey and asked them to join us. We were merely being polite, though they were pretty good-looking, because they had a long wait ahead of them. Well I started giving the better-looking one a big rush to see if she had any possibilities. It was obvious that nothing was going to come of it so when she asked me what we all did I let my imagination carry the ball.

"I'm Sam Lema," I told her. "I've been down here for fifteen years and run a chain of shoe stores. Lema shoes."

The girl seemed to be a little dubious since the quality of my Spanish hardly matched the length of my stay in Puerto Rico. Don Whitt was staring at us a bit dumbfounded and when she asked him what he did for a living he was caught without a snappy comeback. He didn't know whether to go along with the gag or blab the truth. Finally, I guess, he decided he might as well play along. But it was difficult.

"I'm a . . , I'm a . . , I'm a . . ," he began stammering. "I'm an international playboy." This broke me and the other man up, but the poor girls couldn't figure out what kind of nuts we were.

Later Don was a bit peeved that I had put him on the spot like that.

"What the heck were you trying to pull?" he asked me.

"Oh hell," I said. "They didn't want to hear about us being pro golfers. Who would be interested in that?"

"What the hell is wrong with being a pro golfer?" asked the man who had just won two golf tournaments in a row.

Before the week was over even the usually calm and collected Pete Cooper had blown his stack. For a number of campaigns south of the border Pete was called the King of the Caribbean because he won so many tournaments on the Caribbean circuit as well as the special Seagram Trophy and the $2500 check that goes to the man whose overall performance on the tour is the best. Pete was only forty-seven years old, but he trudged slowly along the fairway like a farmer coming in from a hard day behind the plow. Pete is a very sound player with a smooth, effortless swing, but his biggest advantage was the fact that he had been raised in Florida where they had the same kind of stubbly, Bermuda grass greens. Most of us would stand shaking over our putts, afraid to draw back the putter, but Pete would just glide over to it and give the ball the same firm whack he would deliver to a boy who had been caught smoking.

At Panama he won the tournament easily even though only two months before he had had a mild heart attack. He shuffled around the course as if each step would be his last, wearing a wide-brimmed Panama hat and staring out owlishly through a pair of tinted eyeglasses. His son Jerry, a professional at a club in Michigan, was also on the tour, and helped him out quite a bit. Jerry would hold up an umbrella to shield Pete from the strong Caribbean sun and he would often give him a hand up some of the hills. This kind of assistance didn't seem quite kosher to a lot of us, but after all, Pete had been sick and so no one said anything about it. That is until a big flare up occurred at the conclusion of the final round in San Juan.

Ernie Vossler was paired with Pete during the last round and had a chance to pick up a pretty good check until his game suddenly went sour and he finished with a 76.

"All I could see every time I got over the ball," Ernie said later, "was Jerry Cooper standing there with that bright-colored umbrella. He was not only shading his old man from the sun, he was also cleaning Pete's ball on the greens."

Vossler figured enough was enough and that Coop had violated rule 37-2 of the *Rules of Golf* which states: "The player may have only one caddie, under penalty of disqualification." Ernie circled the rule in his own rule book with a pencil, showed it to Pete and then handed it to George Hall. If Ernie's nerves had been a little less frazzled he probably wouldn't have bothered, but he also felt he had an obligation to the rest of the players in the tournament to uphold the rules.

Pete seems like a pretty laconic sort of man, but when stung he has a hornet's temper. I recall an evening at the Tamanaco in Caracas when Jerry Cooper, whose expenses in the Caribbean Pete was paying, had ordered an extra piece of cake for dessert. The father had scolded the son for his extravagance and the son had snapped back. Pete was shocked.

"Are you drunk son?" he growled loudly. "You must be to give lip to your Daddy that way."

Now Pete figured that he had been accused of cheating and he wasn't about to let the charge stand unchallenged. He looked for Ernie after he had put away his clubs, found him sitting by the scoreboard just off the eighteenth hole and, with an audience of some pretty shocked spectators, told him off in good, strong Florida Everglades language. Soon after, they had both calmed down and shaken hands, and the incident was shuffled into the background if not forgotten. That is why I always tell any player about to go on the Caribbean tour that he is going to get tired, that the heat and the banging around are going to jar his nerves, but that he should keep himself under control nonetheless. He is on foreign soil, after all, and should never do anything or say anything, no matter how furious or indignant he may feel, that he could conceivably regret later. At Puerto Rico in 1961 only Billy Maxwell seemed, despite his unorthodox greeting at the airport, to have kept himself under control. He won the tournament by seven shots over De Vicenzo with a very nice 273.

But even Maxwell began to slip a little. At Jamaica he told off one of his archenemies, a photographer, and was fined $50 by George Hall. Jim Ferree won the tournament by six shots and even Don and I started to play pretty well again. Kingston has been replaced on the tour by a stop at Colombia, but it was always a good place to end up because it is such a subdued, restful town. Or should be. It is the capital and commercial center of the island and lacks the gilt and glitter of the plush north shore resorts like Montego Bay and Ocho Rios. After the tournament was over we injected our own form of excitement by putting on a very special kind of golf clinic for the gallery that remained. We were all a bit high and if nobody learned any golf they at least got some laughs. My first job was to demonstrate 2-iron shots and I hit them so badly that three of them together wouldn't have added up to one good wedge. Don Whitt was called out to demonstrate the 4-wood and almost fanned one shot completely, barely topping the ball off the tee. We kidded and tricked each other with the boisterous release of men who have just completed a long, arduous chore — which we had. Most of us can hit a 6-iron, say, about 160 to 170 yards. Well, when it came my turn to demonstrate this club I sneaked a 4-iron, which can hit a ball about 190 yards, out of my bag instead. The next man up, assigned to demonstrate the 5-iron, looked like a weakling to the spectators who observed his 5-irons falling way short of my "6-irons."

All of the players were pretty worn out after the tournament and headed for bed early. I was full of beans, however, and stayed out partying until 4:30 A.M. When I got back to our motel, the Courtleigh Manor, I was in just the right mood to have a little joke at the expense of my pooped-out fellow pros. I slipped a couple of pounds into the hand of the night desk clerk and persuaded him to ring up each room, telling the players that he was instructed to get them up at 5 A.M. to make their flight back to Miami. Well the plane didn't leave until late in the morning and the screaming and shouting could be heard all the way to the Kingston docks. People were still grousing about the hotel's inefficiency as we boarded the plane and made our departure from the Caribbean. I had to join the chorus too. If anyone had suspected my role in this prank I would have been flung through the emergency exit.

When we climbed off the plane in Miami our pockets were loaded with watches and our golf bags with liquor, perfume, bolts of cloth and trinkets of various sorts. Customs fees could have been a severe problem, but we may have avoided a close inspection by pulling out a couple of packages of golf balls and thrusting them into an inspector's hand. I'm sure he felt very kindly to us after this example of our generosity. At the close of the 1961 Caribbean trip Whitt decided to go straight home to his wife and children in San Diego, but I resolved to stay on and play at St. Petersburg. I felt my game was in shape and that I might recover some of the form I had shown in 1958. The last I saw of Don for a month was in the main lobby of Miami International Airport. I had given him a lot of my stuff to take home to the coast and he was staggering under enough liquor, luggage and loot in general to load up a caravan. I shouted goodbye to him as he went out to the plane, told him not to break any of my stuff or I'd charge him for it, and hopped a plane to St. Petersburg.

The past five weeks had been rewarding from several important standpoints. I certainly felt that my game had improved. I had gone back to the fundamental grip I had used in 1958 instead of the fading grip that had fouled me up so badly in 1959 and 1960. I had not won a tournament as I had hoped to, but I had gotten plenty of practice, had played some notably good rounds and gained a great deal of experience. If I couldn't start now living up to the promise I had shown in 1958, well I never would.

# 9 / Lovely towns and lively times

THE 1961 St. Petersburg Open was an ideal tournament at which to turn over a new leaf. Two years before I had a temper tantrum late the final day, taking an 11 on one hole by hastily but intentionally nine-putting the green. I had shot 66 the first day to lead the tournament that year, but had followed this with two 76's and an 84 and finished 27 strokes behind winner Cary Middlecoff. But this was 1961 and it was a new Tony Lema. We were also playing on a different golf course.

This was the Pasadena Golf Club (an unusual name for a Florida course) and it played particularly easy that March. The course was in excellent condition, but there had been very little rain in recent weeks and the fairways were quite hard. This meant that the ball would always roll a long, long way when you hit it reasonably straight. I started the tournament with a par 71, which placed me well back among the also-rans, but I followed this with three of the best rounds I had ever shot in a professional tournament up to that time. I scored a 66 on the second day and then followed that with a 68 and another 66. These rounds jumped me into a tie for thirteenth place and I took away a check for $590. Considering the state I had been in when I left the tour just six weeks earlier, this was a very encouraging return. I packed up my clubs and headed for Miami Beach. I looked forward to another good showing in the Sunshine Open, but I didn't know I would have to contend with life at the Miami Racquet Club.

During the course of the year the pro tour hits a few pretty dull places and many very lively ones. For example at the Waco Turner Open, played in Burneyville, Oklahoma, the week is an exceedingly restful one. Waco Turner is an ardent golf buff and oilman who puts on a tournament at his lodge and country club each year the week the Tournament of Champions is being held in Las Vegas. Since the Las Vegas tournament invites only tournament winners of the past year we refer to Waco's event as the Tournament of Non-champions. It is held on one of the most unusual golf courses in the U.S. I don't recall seeing a sand trap on the entire layout. The first nine holes look like nothing more than a huge flat field with nine mounds on it. These are the putting greens. Each hole, however, is monstrously long. You need two long shots on practically every one to reach one of these greens and there is usually a good, stiff breeze to contend with. The second nine is also long, but it at least contains a few hills and trees.

The tournament is a fine event, however, for the players who haven't qualified for Las Vegas. Overall prize money is $20,000, but Turner antes up an extra $15 bonus for every birdie a player makes, $50 for eagles and $25 every time someone chips in from off the green. He also books the players at his lodge for practically nothing. Since the town of Burneyville consists of about four wooden shacks, a post office and a general store there is not much for the players to do except sit in the clubhouse drinking and playing cards. Unless he is a rotten card player it is easy for a golfer to save his money in Burneyville.

One day I had some washing I needed done and the nearest

launderette turned out to be in Marietta. As launderettes go it was unique. It consisted of a long line of women standing over wash pails with scrubbing boards in their hands. This is life on the glamourous pro tour for one week a year at least.

The difference between Waco Turner's Lodge and the Miami Racquet Club is the difference between a rowboat and Cleopatra's barge. After finishing thirteenth in the 1961 St. Petersburg Open I got down to Miami Beach and checked into the Racquet Club late at night. My room looked directly out on the swimming pool and the next morning when I woke up I could hear the sounds of girlish laughter and the splash of dainty bodies leaping into the water. I peeked through the curtains and there beheld four or five extremely lush little feminine morsels. I knew immediately that this was going to be a good week, if not a very good golfing week. The Racquet Club has several tennis courts and a big swimming pool, and sits right next to one of the canals on the Intracoastal Waterway. Several of the other players, married and single, were staying there, but the single men, naturally, had most of the fun. The married players could only look on enviously and occasionally join us for a drink if we asked them. A good-sized group of golfers, including Bob Rosburg, Gerry Priddy, Mike Souchak and Jay Hebert were staying there. The week was one long party, at least for me. Jay must have been pretty slow getting acquainted because he led the tournament for two days before he blew up and shot 75. I'd have breakfast by the pool, rush over to the golf course to get the business of playing golf over with as quickly as possible, and return to the Racquet Club in time to begin the afternoon's drinking and sunbathing by the pool. We'd have dinner in the dining room, by the pool or even at one of the yachts moored at the club's boat basin. I even took a few tennis lessons, just to get close to the girl who was giving them. The courts were right on the water and when she tapped one across the net to me I'd get a big charge out of teeing off on it and rifling the ball high over the wire screening and out into the canal. My tennis lessons, therefore, came to quite a bit of money since I had to pay for the tennis balls too. But it was worth it. I never learned much about tennis from the pro, but she was a terrific dancer.

One night several of us were sitting alongside the canal having our usual late afternoon cocktails. No one could figure out how wide the canal was, but one of the group bet he could knock the ball over the water with a 7-iron. Jay was would be the one. Well, he had no idea how wide the canal there, myself, Bob Rosburg and Gerry Priddy. Someone said that if anyone could do it, Gerry, with his big, wild swing, was so he got a little too tensed up, took a couple of thrashes at it and dumped two shots right into the water. I was feeling lively enough to have somewhat more courage than I ordinarily do, so, with some of the pretty girls there looking on, I took the club, put the ball in a nice, fluffy lie, and sent a shot high out over the canal and on to the opposite shore. The girls all cheered like mad. Gerry, with the confidence of knowing it could be done, and no doubt inspired by the cheerleaders just as I was, teed a ball up and really slugged it. It went way over the water, high over a house on the other side of the water, and even over some trees on the far side of the house. He had hit the 7-iron a good 210 yards at least.

The Racquet Club is probably my own particular favorite, though the tour seldom stops at Miami Beach anymore, but I guess most of the players prefer Las Vegas, during the Tournament of Champions. The event is sponsored by the Desert Inn, and a player who has won any PGA cosponsored event during the twelve months preceding the Tournament of Champions automatically receives an invitation. Every entrant is guaranteed a minimum of $1000 and the winner's prize is now in the $13,000 vicinity. The Desert Inn hosts the touring pros, and their wives, free of charge. They must figure it will pour right back in the casinos. Well, we all gamble, go to shows at the huge, plush Strip nightclubs, and get very little sleep. The milk drinkers are the winners in Las Vegas.

At many of the stops we can often manufacture our own fun. We used to play a little tournament in Hesperia, California, every year. It was a week in which a lot of the players let down their hair and had a ball. The feature entertainment was a jam session that the players put on at the club when they got through playing golf; Lionel Hebert on the trumpet, Ken Venturi on the drums, Murray Arnold on the piano and Don Whitt and myself on the bass. Of course, I can't play the bass at all, but I would get roped into it every now and then if Whitt wasn't around, or wanted a break for a drink. I could slap at it and make some noise. We always had a terrific time.

Ken and I both regard the Indianapolis tournament as one of our favorites. It always takes place in late May and the whole week, climaxed by the race, is one big celebration. The streets are jammed with parades and the nightclubs and restaurants with movie stars. First rate films are playing at the local theaters.

The golf course is, in fact, an integral part of the race in that nine of its holes are located in the huge infield of the track. We play the first three holes outside the track, cross underneath through a tunnel and then play the fourth through twelfth holes, cross underneath again and finish the last six holes outside the track. One year the carburetor trials were being held while we were playing our practice rounds. It was quite a test in concentration. Try to putt sometime just when an Offenhauser is roaring by at 150 mph.

Johnny Boyd, who has raced at Indianapolis a number of years, comes from San Francisco and is a good friend of Ken Venturi. Knowing Johnny has simply sharpened the pleasure we get from watching the Indianapolis "500," and both Ken and I have gone to extravagant lengths to be there during race day.

Memorial Day, 1962, fell on a Wednesday, three days after the end of the Indianapolis Open and just prior to the Memphis Open. Ken and I were also scheduled to qualify for the U.S. Open at a course in Memphis. Immediately after playing at Indianapolis Ken and I flew to Memphis. On Monday we played a practice round at the Memphis Country Club, where the Open qualifying was to be held. On Tuesday we went over to the Colonial Country Club, where the Memphis Open is held, and played a practice round. On Tuesday night we hopped back to Indianapolis, watched the race on Wednesday, and were back in Memphis in time to tee off Thursday morning. By that time we both felt as if we too had raced in the Indianapolis "500."

One thing that can make any town exciting, of course, is the girls. Where women are concerned the problem for even a moderately successful touring pro is not to hunt them down but to weed them out. This is true not only in golf, but also in baseball, football or even the entertainment world. There is something about being in the limelight, performing in front of large crowds, of being sought after and attended, that makes a man seem exciting and suggestive to a great many women. This is very distinctly one of the not-so-fringe benefits of being a touring pro. When he is playing well and getting into the newspapers a touring pro can have his pick of the girls.

On the golf tour, and it must be pretty much true along the other professional sports routes, the girls seem to fall into about four categories, most of them pretty easy to spot right off. In the first category are the girls who simply want to be seen with a sports celebrity because they figure some of the attention being lavished on him will wash off on her. She is a celebrity hound. She wants to bask in his fame and thinks by so doing she becomes a big deal herself. This type of babe will give you the big, sexy hello and the big eye and promise you anything. The trouble is she doesn't even give you Arpège. The best thing to do with this girl is plead a sick headache and take her home early.

In a second category are the golf-nutty girls. They would go out with a two-headed, six-handed gorilla if he could play a good game of golf. Some of these are very pleasant and really want to learn more about the game. Others just want to talk golf, golf, golf when you clearly have some other activity in mind. Here again, the sick-headache play is probably the best way out.

Third, there is the large category of normal, well-bred women who see you not as a golfer or a celebrity but just as a man. These girls are at least moderately interested in golf because they will be traveling in golfing circles, but this fact is not going to help you score with them, necessarily. They are the type of girl you might meet any time and anywhere.

The final category includes the impulsive, aggressive types. They make no bones of the fact that they are out to have a good time and they figure a touring pro is the best kind of guy to have it with. You run into them out on the course during a round. A colorfully dressed tomato, usually a pretty good-looking one with a lot of confidence, will be standing on the path that leads from the green of one hole to the tee of the next. She will have to move out of your way as you go by and so you can't help noticing her. She may also stand in a conspicuous place alongside the fairway or you may bump into her trying to get a drink at a water fountain. If for some reason or other she misses you when your round of golf is finished she has a very good way of getting hold of you: the telephone. Throughout my first five years on the tour, while I was a bachelor, there were many times when little scenes like this were played out.

Just for purposes of supplying a typical example let's say that the tour is playing the Orange Country Open during my bachelor days. I am alone in my room, stretched out on the bed and watching television. The phone beside my bed rings. I pick it up.

"Hello," I say.

"Hello, Tony?" a girl's voice at the other end of the phone asks.

"Yes," I say.

"My name is so-and-so and I was in your gallery today," the girl says. "Do you remember? I was wearing a bright green dress with a yellow bandana and pink golf shoes and you said hello to me on your way to the twelfth tee."

"Oh, yes," I might say, sometimes recalling the girl or the incident and sometimes not.

"Well, I was just here in the bar downstairs," says the girl, "and I thought I'd give you a call and say hello. What are you doing?"

"I'm watching television."

"Good program?"

"Yes. I think you'd like it."

[ 146 ]

"Well . . . . that's nice."

"Why don't you come on up and watch it with me."

"Okay."

It doesn't take much imagination to fill out the rest of this scene, which is very typical of what can take place.

However you meet them women are the breath of fresh air that can cool off the hot competitive climate of the pro tour, and relieve its tedium. They not only call you up on the phone from the lobby of your motel, or congratulate you on a good round in the country club grill. You meet them everywhere. In Greensboro, Fred Koury, who runs the Plantation Room not too far from the golf course, always somehow manages to have a lot of attractive girls in his restaurant. In St. Paul there is a hospitality room for the players in the St. Paul Hotel where you can meet girls from the airlines, or various beauty-contest entrants. It is often a contest between the single pros to see who can score. In Las Vegas, of course, the variety of girls is endless. It is hard to get to bed early in that town.

Where women are concerned the liveliest spots, at least for a single man, are the places I mentioned above plus Dallas, the airline-stewardess heaven; Miami, which is always swarming with vacationers looking for a good time; Phoenix, for the same reason; Los Angeles, Chicago, New York, New Orleans and San Francisco. The Bing Crosby pro-am always draws the beauties.

In general good-looking girls just seem to turn up at a country club when a golf tournament is in progress, but you can hit some pretty dry wells, too. Some of the more sedate places include Tucson, Pensacola, maybe Boston, though I've only played in the latter city once and never as a bachelor.

Even considering all the lovely women he runs into, life on the pro tour can still be a pretty lonely business for a bachelor.

[ 147 ]

I had my five years of bachelorhood and don't regret a second of it, but I would never trade it for marriage now. I'm very much in love and very happy with my wife Betty and my life has been completely changed. I feel I am a better person, a more complete person and even a better golfer. I'm now playing for someone besides myself. I've got a wife to make happy, a slew of kids yet to come and I feel I want to build something for them. Naturally, I took an awful lot of kidding when I first got married just as did a lot of the touring bachelors — Bob Goalby, Jim Ferree, numerous others — when they made the same move. Everyone was watching very carefully to see how I'd play.

At the 1963 Tournament of Champions the early line established by the bookmakers gave me a six to one chance against winning. When the word got out that I was planning to get married and take my honeymoon in Las Vegas while playing in the tournament, the odds on me tumbled to fifteen to one. I don't know whether those odds had any takers, but I played well in spite of what might be considered adverse circumstances and anyone backing me to show would have made money.

The next week I finished fifth at Colonial, then won at Memphis, tied for second at Indianapolis and finished in the top ten at the Buick Open despite having a first-round, five under par 67, rained out. As Arnold Palmer said right after I had tied him in the Tournament of Champions, maybe we should all get married every week. To the same girl, of course.

# 10 / *Comeback with a putter*

THE modest comeback that the 1961 St. Pete Open had at least hinted was in progress continued for me right into June. I was thinking well, playing well and picking up some very nice checks. Official money means two things on the pro tour. First of all, just like anyone, we can spend it. Secondly, it is also a measure of accomplishment, like a batting average in baseball or a points-per-game average in basketball. A player's rank on the money-earned list can have a significant effect on his tournament program, at least at the middle levels. This is because any golfer among the top forty on the official list in the year's final money statistics is exempt from pre-tournament qualifying the following year. He is thus spared the frustration of the Ghost Squadron. He also gets an automatic ticket to the special invitational tournaments like the Colonial Invitational in Fort Worth, the American Golf Classic, the Sahara Invitational in Las Vegas, and other tournaments that fill out their field by invitation only and do not even have pre-event qualifying. Being in the top forty also means that the player is invited to compete in pro-amateur tournaments. It has reached the point on the tour where practically every event is now preceded by a pro-am that will distribute from $2000 to $10,000 in prize money to the forty pros who compete in them. These pro-ams are almost always held the day before the tournament proper begins. In such an event each pro is paired with three amateurs and two tournaments are going on simultaneously. The top six or eight teams, on a best-ball basis will earn money for their pro members; the top eight or ten pros, on the basis of their individual scores, will also pick up checks. First prize in each category pays between $250 and $1000. This is unofficial money, but it can still be a pretty nice source of income.

At the beginning of 1961 I was struggling hard to pick up enough checks to get into the top forty on the official lists — even though the five weeks I had spent in the Caribbean did not count officially — and I was doing pretty well until, suddenly, I ran into a severe case of the putting jitters. They got so bad that I began to think the only solution would be to get out of tournament golf altogether. I was not going to let a thing like putting ruin my entire life. I would quit golf first.

I had started taking between 38 and 40 putts per round, some six or eight more than the 32 putts most of us consider about right for a consistent game of golf. I was never able to hole a four-footer for a par and I'd usually come up with about five or six three-putt greens a round. I had not qualified for the U.S. Open that year and so after the Memphis tournament I went up to Detroit and borrowed a car from a close friend of mine, Ed Addis, for the three and a half hour drive to Grand Rapids, where the Western Open was being held. At Grand Rapids I combined bad playing with my usual bad putting, missed the 36-hole cutoff and headed back for Detroit. I was going to drop the car off at Addis's house, pack up my clubs and clothes and head home. Ed was not there and so I sat down to wait for his return. While I was waiting it occurred to me that Detroit was the home of Horton Smith, the pro at the Detroit Country Club, and one of the game's great putters. I had met him a couple of years before, decided now that I would call him up with the hope that he would remember me and be willing to do something about the sad state of my putting stroke. I looked up the number of the club in the directory, dialed the number and soon he was on the line.

"Hello, Mr. Smith," I said. "This is Tony Lema. Do you remember that we met a couple of years ago?"

"Sure, I remember, Tony," he said. "How are you?"

"Well, I'm not too good," I said. "My putting is shot to pieces, and unless it gets put together again I'm just going to have to quit the tour. I was hoping that you might be able to help me."

"Absolutely," he said. "You come right on over. I'm sure all you've lost is your confidence, but you come over and we'll get that confidence back again for you and get you back to a good putting stroke." I felt better almost as soon as I had set the telephone back in its cradle. I drove over to Horton's club and for an hour we practiced on the putting green. He talked to me about what a putting stroke should be and what I could do about smoothing out mine. I could feel the confidence ebbing back into me as he talked. Horton explained that putting was almost entirely a right-handed stroke and that the left hand was there only to help keep the blade on line. He demonstrated an extremely helpful exercise. This involved holding the putter with nothing but my right hand and hitting the ball at the hole from two feet, then four feet, then six and finally 10 feet. My stroke came back. It was a miracle. Horton couldn't have been more considerate and I can never thank him enough for what he did. His sudden death in 1963 was a tragic loss to golf. He was the only man I know who ever put more into the game of golf than he took out of it. I felt so eager that I jumped right back into Addis's car and drove up to Flint, Michigan, where the Buick Open was being held.

In the Buick Open I started out with a 71 and a 72, pretty good golf on the longest course the tour hits each year (7300 yards). I started hitting the ball badly over the last two rounds and finished with a 75 and a 77, but still was high up enough to earn $200. My putting had been wonderful. I felt I could eventually become a very good putter.

Next stop: St. Paul. I shot three fair rounds and one very good one, tied for fifteenth and picked up a check for $670. I was so pleased with my showing in the tournament that I gave a party in my suite at the St. Paul Hotel. A bunch of us were taking the train that night to Winnepeg, where we would play in the Canadian Open. Since the train was a late one I invited a few of the players and some girls I had met in the hotel's Hospitality Room, and we celebrated until train time. It was a delightful evening. Before it ended we were teeing golf balls up on the rug and driving them out the window and over what must have been a very surprised city of St. Paul.

Next stop: Winnipeg and the Canadian Open. I shot a first-round 65 to lead the tournament by a shot over Jacky Cupit, who eventually won it, Jon Gustin and Bob Pratt. I couldn't match Cupit after that — he finished 69, 64, 71 — but I tied for seventh with a 277 and earned $1250.

Next stop: Milwaukee. I closed with a burst, shooting a final-round 66 to tie for sixth place at 275 with Tom Nieporte, Gary Player and a young amateur named Jack Nicklaus. My putting was very good, but I was also beginning to learn at last the secret I had searched for vainly way back in December, 1957, at the Mayfair Inn Open when after my third round I had gone out to watch some of the top stars play. At that time I thought that their consistency was due entirely to experience. Milwaukee supplied me with rather dramatic proof that week-in, week-out consistency came as much from the mind as from the golf swing. I started the last round in eighteenth place, tied with Tom Nieporte, Venturi and two other lesser-known players. We were all at 209, eight shots back of leader Bruce Crampton. After 10 holes I was three under par and had closed to within three or four shots of Crampton and actually felt I had a good chance to catch him. Then I bogeyed the eleventh, twelfth and thirteenth holes, right in a row, to throw my fine round right out the window. I thought to myself, "Goddamnit, what are you doing now? You're always blowing up like this." On the fourteenth hole I missed a very short putt that would have given me a birdie. I was just about to whirl and put my putter into orbit in the general direction of the clubhouse. I checked myself in time. It wasn't the putter's fault, particularly, and I began talking to myself as I walked to the fifteenth tee. I said, "Tony, wait until you have played the last four holes before you get mad. Then when you get into the clubhouse break all your clubs, smash them, twist them into metal pretzels, do anything you want. But while you're out here see what you can salvage. You only have four holes to play and it will only take an hour." Well, it wasn't just a coincidence that I finished with four straight birdies, jumped back into a tie for sixth and picked up a check for $1300. The eighteenth was particularly memorable. It was a par five that could be reached with two good shots. but I hit my tee shot into deep grass. Trying to really smash the second shot and get it onto the green I succeeded only in knocking it to the right and under a tree about 80 yards short of the green. I was partially stymied by the tree trunk, and a low branch forced me to play the ball low. I choked up on a 5-iron and cut across the ball on the shot, sending a low slice out toward the green. The ball hit with a great deal of slicing spin on it, ran toward the green, bounced right around a sand trap and up to eight feet from the hole.

Learning to keep his temper is one thing a touring pro finds very difficult to do, but he absolutely must in order to play consistently good golf. It is not so much the act of blowing up that is harmful, it is the attitude behind the act that does the damage. Golf is a game of so many bounces — up and down, from right to left, backward and forward — that many of these bounces are going to go against the golfer. He must learn to understand that this will happen and then learn to accept these misfortunes with good grace. Otherwise, even if he isn't throwing clubs, shouting at photographers or spectators, he is not going to play his best golf. The sport is definitely one for an unruffled composure.

The constant pressure, the need to bear down on every shot or toss away a potful of prize money, eventually has an unnerving effect on all of us. Tommy Bolt is not the only one capable of tempestuous outbreaks. Golf does not supply the physical release that more active sports like baseball, basketball and football do. This kind of repression inevitably produces a reaction.

When I first came out on the tour the players used to tell me about a trigger-tempered pro named Ivan Gantz who had just left it. "I had been on the tour just a short time when I first laid eyes on Ivan," Don January told me. "I was walking down one fairway and looked over into another and there was this fellow with blood pouring out of a big gash in his forehead. It was Gantz and he had gone and hit himself on the head with his putter." The pros used to tell about how, after missing short putts, Gantz would dive into creeks or sand traps, hit himself over the head with a rock, or roll around in the grass like a dog trying to scrape off fleas.

No one is immune to the urge. I'm not the only golfer who has thrown his bag of clubs into a creek after hitting a bad shot or three-putting a green. Jim Ferree can tell you about the times he has done it. I am also not alone in having taken a half dozen extra putts on a green. In the 1963 Phoenix Open I was paired with Dave Hill and at the ninth hole he first hit a shot high up into a palm tree, where it stayed, then knocked two more shots out-of-bounds. By the time we had reached the green Dave was as hot as a hornet. When it came his turn to putt he simply chased his ball across the green, hitting it again and again as it rolled — at two penalty strokes per whack. Dave made a nice fat score of 15 on the ninth hole in that round.

The right idea, of course, is not only never to lose your temper while you are playing golf, but not even to *feel* like losing it. This is an impossible goal to achieve, but the nearer a golfer can get to it the more effective a player he will be.

As the 1961 season began to draw to a close this was the state of mind I had begun to achieve. Through the fall I began to finish among the top ten or fifteen in almost every tournament. I won the 36-hole Hesperia Open, took a vacation from the tour for a few weeks, went to Mexico City where I won the Mexican Open, then returned and picked up the tour at Florida in December. I finished eleventh at West Palm Beach, and at the Coral Gables Open — the last event of the year — I finished in the money and so managed to qualify for the Los Angeles Open. My putting was sound, so was my temperament, and I was knocking at the door of my first big tournament victory. I had turned what had started to be a miserable year into a pretty good one. Officially I won $11,505, but unofficial money from pro-ams and the Caribbean tour had given me a total income of well over $20,000. I felt so confident about my future that a sponsor to back me on the tour fell into the category of a non-essential item. Crocker had promised me my freedom from our contract whenever I wanted it. So as the 1962 campaign got underway I asked him if we might not end our arrangement, with only the stipulation that I would pay back the approximately $11,000 debt that I had compiled during my lean years. Life looked rosy once again and sullen Tony Lema no longer needed lectures from his friends to get him to behave like a normal, cheerful adult.

# 11 / *Let a protégé beware*

WE never used to argue about it too heatedly, but **Tommy** Jacobs and I disagreed on the subject of whether pro golfers should start out with sponsors. I was pro and Tommy was con, but recent experience has caused me to reevaluate my stand quite a bit. Practically every rookie coming out on the tour these days has a surefire method of financing himself for at least a year. In the first place the PGA would never approve his Player's card if he didn't. In the second place he might not be able to eat. Most of the players are backed by a person or group of persons who provide them with enough money to pay expenses. The usual agreement is for the player to pay back all the money he has been advanced and to split all earnings above that amount with his sponsors. Usually all the sponsor ever does is put up the cash. He seldom acts as the player's manager, or business or press agent.

The first time this method of financing ever gained much publicity was back in 1957 when San Diego's Billy Casper started to win golf tournaments and make a lot of money. Casper was backed by two Chula Vista, California, businessmen, Russ Corey and Dick Haas. He repaid their loan plus 30 percent of his winnings over that amount. The contract ran about four years, by which time Casper was well established on the tour and Corey and Haas had made a little money for themselves.

Dave Ragan had an unusual arrangement when he first came out on the tour in 1957. Dave is from Florida, and a group of sportsmen from Daytona Beach who called themselves the Florida Sports Enterprises, Inc., backed him to the tune of $1000 per month in exchange for the total earnings of his first two years on the tour. This came, officially, to about $10,000.

There must be a million ways of getting financial help. Players like Bo Wininger and Bob McCallister draw salaries doing public relations work for their backers; Bo for an Odessa, Texas, automobile dealer named Bob French, Bob for bandleader Lawrence Welk. Bob Goalby was an assistant pro at the Wee Burn Country Club in Darien, Connecticut, when he decided to come out on the tour in 1958, so club members raised the money to get him started. I also heard of one rookie who must have figured he was quite a wheeler and dealer. Before setting out on the tour he sold shares in himself. Unfortunately he was a little too enthusiastic and sold 125 percent. He exhausted the nest egg soon enough, but every time he won $100 in prize money he had to pay out $125. It was a lot cheaper not to win a dime so he dropped off the tour for a while to do some refinancing.

Tommy Jacobs was one of the few players I met in my early years on the tour who had refused to make any sort of sponsorship deal.

"I'd feel badly if I'd come out on the tour, done badly and not been able to pay my sponsors back," he used to say. "But I'd have felt worse having to shell out to someone else money that I'd won. I just decided I'd better make it on my own."

Tommy had pretty good credentials, however, before he turned pro. At sixteen, back in 1951, he won the National Junior Championship, for boys up to seventeen years old, and the same summer reached the semifinals of the National Amateur that Billy Maxwell won. In his first tournament as a pro, the 1957 Los Angeles Open, Tommy tied for third.

In my early years on the tour I disagreed with Tommy about sponsorships because I felt that for many guys it was the only way of getting started at all. I know I felt I had a very good deal. It just goes to show that before you sign up for a terrific deal you had better know who your friends really are. Crocker, the genial sportsman whom I had met during my year in Elko, must have had more faith in my ability to make it on the tour than I did. He had played golf with me, saw me win the Montana Open and finally, at the urging of pro Cliff Whittle, agreed to finance me on the tour. We were having drinks together at the time and I figured this was nothing but the drinks talking. But the next day Crocker agreed to pay Cliff's and my way to three tournaments that were being held in Southern California during the fall of 1957. They were the 54-hole Hesperia Open, the $20,000 San Diego Open and the 54-hole Long Beach Open. We didn't set any scoring records, the two of us, but we played well and enjoyed ourselves thoroughly. When I got back to Elko I thanked Crocker and then he asked me if I'd really like to try the tour full-time. I said yes, I wouldn't mind trying it. Actually I was a little reluctant, because I wasn't too sure I could make it. I didn't think of it as the great plan for my future or anything like that. What I really wanted to do was simply to get away from Elko, Nevada. I had put in one season there and that was enough. I had boozed too much, fooled around with women too much, and had dumped all my money into Elko's casinos. In fact, I probably would have left sooner if I hadn't gotten up to my ears in debt to the town's gamblers. The tour would be a good life, Crocker seemed like a good guy, and I'd get to see the country. I thought of it almost like a two-year vacation of play with pay.

My original arrangement with Crocker was an oral one. He agreed to send me $200 a week. I made the down payment on a new Plymouth and he was to keep up the rest of the payments. My part of the bargain was to repay the money he advanced and then give him one-third of all my earnings over that amount.

It is not too difficult to figure out why someone, especially a golf nut, agrees to back a player on the pro tour. Often it is an unselfish act made simply to help out a friend. Often it is something else. In the first place it gives the sponsor a sense of participation. He has his horse on the tour. This is almost as much fun as being on it himself. In the second place, he can then come out on the tour, be introduced to the players and pal around with them. Just like one of the boys. Finally, the sponsor can sort of big shot it at home. He is a big generous sportsman who is supporting some worthy boy in the lad's chosen profession. It wasn't until I tried to break the contract that I realized Crocker's motives might involve profit as well.

The Crocker-Lema team did all right during its first year. My partner came out on the tour and traveled with me from time to time. When he was at home I'd call him each week and keep him posted. Sometimes he sent a check for $200, sometimes for $500 and sometimes I had to wait in my hotel until he had wired the money through Western Union. During the year I made about $16,000 counting pro-ams and official tournaments, so Crocker got all his money back. This left a surplus of about $2000, but Crocker was generous and told me to put it in my pocket.

He was going to get me an agent, he was going to get me

publicized, he had a sack full of great ideas. The first step on my way to becoming a businessman was to sign a written contract. The smart thing would have been to end the arrangement right then and there. After all, I had made a good start on the tour and felt that I would do better in 1959. But I wasn't very smart. I thought Crocker was a helluva guy and a good friend. Besides he promised that the contract was just a means for me to get accustomed to the ways of business and that any time I wanted out all I had to do was say the word. The new contract called for me to receive $12,000 a year instead of $200 a week. I was to repay that amount and split earnings over that sum in the same one-third, two-thirds manner that we had the year before. I could also feel free to borrow extra money if I needed it, though this would not affect the base rate for our profit split.

There were two items in the contract that were to make it extremely difficult for me to get anything out of the deal. One was that I was to go first class all the way, sell the car, fly from tournament to tournament, and stay at the best places. No hamburgers for Crocker's boy Tony Lema, just prime filet mignon. This made my playing the tour so expensive that I made him raise the basic advance from $12,000 to $14,000 and then eventually to $16,000. Back home, meanwhile, Crocker was getting a favorable reputation as a big sport who sent his boy first cabin. He was written up in the West Coast papers and even in *Sport* magazine. By the time I had traveled first class all around the country and paid him back, even in my good year of 1962, I didn't have much left for myself. My two bad years of 1959 and 1960 really put me in the hole. Living high was fun, but it was costing me considerably more than I wanted to pay.

A joker in the deal was that I had signed a three-year contract that contained options extending its life through 1966. I was practically tied up for life because the option was something he could exercise, but which I could not. I must have been pretty green in those days, but I did have reassurances that I could forget the options and end the contract any time I wanted to.

Under the first two years of the written contract I made out all right. That is, if you call getting deep into debt making out all right. A clause in the contract required that all debts would be carried forward from year to year. This meant that unless I quit the tour entirely he would eventually get his money back. Well, things got so bad in 1959 and '60 that even Crocker was ready to write off the debt if I would quit the tour. He called me from time to time encouraging this move. I guess he got tired of shelling out and shelling out. I earned a total of $15,000 during those two years and spent a total of $30,000. I carried forward into 1961 a debt of $11,000.

Even my comeback during the third year of the written contract didn't cut into the debt. My total earnings came to about $20,000, but by the time I had met my high expenses and given Crocker his cut there was nothing left. I still had no money at all. I was slowly catching on, however, about what was up so I decided to just forget about these financial problems and go ahead and play golf. At the same time I asked Crocker to end the contract.

This was during July of 1962. I agreed, of course, to pay off anything I owed him at that point. He said, "Okay, I'll have my lawyers draw up the necessary papers and send them along right away." I had gone home. I went to his home city while I was on the coast and sat in his lawyer's office while he instructed him to legally end the contract. Then I went back out on the tour. The papers never arrived. I kept calling him, he kept assuring me they were on their way, but when Christmas rolled around the Christmas present I had been expecting from Crocker since July had still not arrived.

By this time I had begun to click on the tour. In 1962 I had won a couple of tournaments and made a total of $48,000 in official and unofficial money. Unfortunately my expenses had been prodigious, coming to a total of $27,000. Thus the financial picture looked something like this:

| | |
|---|---:|
| Debt carried forward from 1961 | $11,000 |
| Expenses during 1962 (all advanced by Crocker and repaid) | 27,000 |
| One-third of the difference between contracted $16,000 and the total earnings, to be paid to Crocker | 11,000 |
| | ——— |
| Total outgo | $49,000 |
| Total income | $48,000 |
| Left for Tony Lema          minus | $1000 |

The slate had been wiped clean. Crocker, the wealthy, generous sportsman, had gotten his kicks, gotten all his money back and had even made a profit. Then, suddenly, it appeared that Crocker was neither generous nor a sportsman and apparently not even as wealthy as he had led people to believe. He insisted on exercising the options and flatly refused to end the contract. Now I hired my own attorneys. While I played golf the lawyers wrangled.

I was pretty upset and confused by it all but I continued to play pretty good golf and in the first half of 1963 I made over $60,000. Since the contract had not been broken a good hunk of this was going into Crocker's bank account. I postponed signing contracts that would have given me plenty of outside income because I knew very little would be left for me. Finally, the problem became so acute that my golf suffered. I passed up the British Open, the Canadian Open and the Western Open just to stay home and gab with lawyers about my contract. Crocker finally agreed to sell it to me. The total price came to everything I had made in 1963, less expenses, plus an additional $22,000 to be paid over the following two years. Now I was not only flat broke after having earned $110,000 in eighteen months, but I was in hock up to my ears. I'm embarrassed to say what I had to pay Crocker to get out of the contract, but anyone can figure out that it came to a good deal more than $50,000.

In five and a half years on the tour Tony Lema, the golfer, had nothing to show for it while Crocker, the sponsor, had turned a profit of over $60,000. He had never made good on the publicity he promised to produce and he had never gotten me an agent. That might have been too dangerous. But he certainly made good on his promise to teach me something about business. It was a five-and-a-half-year education that cost considerably more than I would have had to pay the Harvard Business School, but I'll never sign another contract, even if it has been drawn up by my mother, without reading the small print. That can be a valuable lesson in itself.

# 12 / *A lesson from show business*

THE fact that I suddenly became a winning golfer in the fall of 1962, after years of being an also-ran and worse, is something that has surprised a great many people. "How do you account for it?" they keep asking me. I have had to make the same explanation a thousand times and after a while I just could not say the same set of words again. "I guess I'm just lucky," is what I finally used for an explanation.

Of course I never believed it was luck alone and my good year of 1963 confirmed this thinking. I matured as a player in 1962 and 1963, but the seed for my success had been planted during the winter of 1960.

I was playing in the Palm Springs Desert Classic that February. This is a very special, very hectic kind of tournament. It was then played over a 90-hole, five-day route, on four of the courses in Palm Springs. One of its most confusing factors is that it is a pro-am. For each of the first four days each pro is paired with a different three-man team of amateurs. The result is three tournaments in one and so much confusion on the crowded courses that players have often found themselves, after completing a hole, heading for the wrong tee.

The first such tournament was played in 1960 and I was there. One of my amateur partners was a fellow named Danny Arnold, a member of the Tamarisk Country Club in Palm Springs and a pretty good player with about a 10-handicap. Danny was a television and movie director-writer-producer who had moved out to the coast from New York about ten years earlier. We hit it off right away. We played together during the first round, I shot a 67 and tied for the first-day lead with Arnold Palmer, Johnny Palmer, Bob Goalby and Mason Rudolph. After our round together Danny invited me to stay with him and his wife Donna while I was in Palm Springs. The Arnolds were just about the warmest, friendliest couple I had ever met. We did a lot of talking that week and I guess we got to know each other pretty well. I had a lot of problems and needed someone to talk to. Danny was a great listener, but he was also a pretty good talker as well.

One of the things Danny Arnold spotted about me pretty quickly was the fact that, while I was overemotional about my golf, I did not have a properly serious attitude about it. These were the dog days in the golfing life of Tony Lema and he could use some straightforward advice about his attitude toward the game. The first thing Danny tried to do was build up my confidence. The greatest golfer in the world is nothing without confidence, while with it a usually mediocre player can be awfully hard to beat. He started out by telling me what a fine swing he thought I had and what a basically fine player I was. One round of golf was all anyone needed in those days to see what kind of temper I had. Danny started trying to convince me that temper tantrums never would work *for* me, only against me. I wasn't really hard to convince, it was simply that I didn't have the self-control to discipline myself. After I missed a short putt I knew it was wrong to do so, but I would often step to the next tee and almost deliberately try to rifle my drive out of bounds. I was only punishing myself, of course, but I guess that was the purpose. I had missed a short putt, now I was to be punished for missing it. Simple, yet foolish.

My bad habits were well ingrained so I was hardly a new man when it was time to leave the Arnolds in Palm Springs and head for Phoenix, but I had made a start, Whenever I was in the Los Angeles or Palm Springs area the Arnolds and I would get together. Between visits, I called him on the telephone to let him know how things were going and how I was feeling.

My visits to Danny's house in Palm Springs were always enjoyable, mostly because the Arnolds were such pleasant people, but also because they usually had a houseful of interesting guests. Through his work in the movies and in television Danny naturally had made a great many friends in the entertainment business. One of them was Danny Kaye, a very ardent golfer who gave up the game for a while to take up flying, but is now back on the golf course. He is a very good golfer, getting the same smooth, unforced rhythm into his golf swing that he gets into his dancing. He shoots in the 70's and seems to play just as well under pressure in a big pro-amateur as he does just fooling around.

At dinner one night we were all talking about show business and I made the rather stupid observation that being an actor must be one of the world's easiest professions.

"That's right," Kaye said. "If you have the guts for it."

That made a lot of sense to me. Maybe I could become half the golfer that Kaye was a showman if I could just get the courage to control my temper. I also asked Kaye how he prepared himself to go on the stage. People sometimes take for granted that an entertainer — or a golfer — will just go out on the stage and produce a bang-up show. I suspected that there was more to it than that, because I knew just teeing it up wasn't all that was involved in playing tournament golf. Yes, he said, there were plenty of obstacles to overcome, just as there were in anything, and the first step was to make up your mind that you were going to clear them. When he was preparing for a show Kaye would always try to get into the nightclub, the theater or the auditorium while someone else was on and wander around, just trying to get the feel of the place and of the acoustics. He also made a point of being in the hall when it was empty. He found this reassuring when it was time to go on stage before a tremendous crowd.

The more people from his world that I met in Danny Arnold's house the more I began to realize why there is such an affinity between show people and golfers on the tour. We are all performers, of course, and a mutual admiration society seems to have developed. There is an interchange in dress and in lingo that goes on all the time. The tour spends a great part of the year at tournaments in California and so this semi-cultural exchange is stimulated even further. Bing Crosby has been putting on his pro-celebrity-amateur tournament since before World War II and Pebble Beach during the Crosby Clambake is always crawling with show business people. I couldn't ever trace it directly, but I strongly suspect that some of the lingo of the tour comes from such voluble and imaginative performers as Bob Hope and Phil Harris, both devoted golfers. I doubt if phrases like "rammycackle" — meaning to really tee off on a shot — originated on the pro tour. Other expressions that seem to be made in Hollywood are: Sunset Strip — a score of 77; trombones — a score of 76; jollywopped one — rammycackled it; a driver with a cashmere inlay — the ball has been hit hard, but does not go very far.

Tournament golf has also become tremendously popular as a television attraction. About a dozen events a year are televised live and these are supplemented by several filmed shows. Sometimes you can't tell the golfers from the comedians. Gary Player and Phil Rodgers are two of the tour's biggest hams. They have made showmanship a fine art. Phil will march double-time around a green after he has holed a sizable putt — and he makes plenty of that variety — clap his hands wildly in self-applause and then run up to the hole and throw his cap over it. Gary is fully as energetic as Phil. One of his specialties is to crouch on the green and then kick out one leg like a chorine. He can also Indian dance on the green, leap high into the air when a putt drops or scale his cap skyward. He once showed up for the British Open wearing a pair of slacks that had one black leg and one white one.

# 13 / *Help from a touring caddy*

Until I met Danny Arnold, however, about the only acting I ever had a chance to do was bad acting. His constant advice, the firsthand evidence gained from tournament play that his advice worked, and I guess just the fact that I was getting older and a little more mature, finally brought my volatile temperament under control. By 1962 the results were beginning to show in rather dramatic fashion. I played pretty well during my second trip through the Caribbean. When I got back the Doral Open, played at Miami in March, supplied another important tip-off.

The Doral Country Club course is probably one of the toughest we play on the tour. It pays a first prize of $9000 and always draws the very best players. During the first round of the 1962 Doral tournament I fired a big, fat 82. Ordinarily a first-round score like that would have finished me for the week. Not only because I would have had trouble making the 36-hole cutoff, but also because I would have been too mad or too depressed to bother playing well after that. At Doral, however, I stuck to my guns, played three good rounds and, while 82's aren't ever going to put you in contention for the lead in a tournament, managed to squeeze into the money. I felt quite proud of myself on that occasion, but there were also others. I was driving badly at the U.S. Open and missed the cut, but the following week at Baltimore, in the Eastern Open, I recovered from a first-round 75 to finish third just two shots back of winner Doug Ford. Then at the Buick Open, two weeks later, I got about as bad a break as I have ever had in golf. Bill Collins, the big, blond long-hitter from Baltimore, Pete Cooper, the King of the Caribbean, and myself were tied for the lead at 212 going into the final round. I was paired with Pete and Jim Ferree in the very last threesome on the course, with Collins just out in front of us. The second hole at the Warwick Hills Country Club in Flint, Michigan, is a par five that bends around trees to the right. It is possible, by cutting the corner on one's second shot, to land right in front of the green and thus give yourself a great chance for a birdie four. In this final round I had put my drive in perfect position to fly my second shot over the trees and up near the green. In an attempt to do so I hit what I thought was a truly fine 5-iron shot. I looked up in time to see the ball soaring toward the top of a tree right at the corner. I figured that even if it nicked the tree I wouldn't have any trouble because the branches were extremely thin way up there. Suddenly the ball hit something that must have been as solid as a brick wall. It caromed straight left, high across the fairway, and clean out of bounds on the opposite side. I was shocked and heartbroken.

"Son," said Pete, who was as surprised as I at the turn of events, "that's the worst piece of luck I have ever seen a man have on a golf course."

That was something I didn't need to be told. I was now two over par on a golf course that eats players alive. A year earlier a break like that would have had me throwing clubs and hitting shots in all directions. This time I decided just to work as hard as I could for the next 16 holes and hope that something good would come of it. I finished two over par in that stretch for a 76 and an eventual tie for sixth, but I felt a strong sense of satisfaction and picked up a check for $1825 as well. Danny's constant encouragement had paid off, if not with a tournament victory, at least with the promise of one.

I remember a couple of other tournaments that year with special sharpness. A first-round 77 in the Oklahoma City Open and then a rally that put me into a tie for fourth. A final-round 63 in the Seattle Open that might have won the tournament for me had I not been bogeying the seventy-first hole while Jack Nicklaus, the eventual winner playing behind me, had been scoring an eagle three on the sixty-ninth hole at the same moment. Going into the last round I had been in fourteenth place, seven shots behind Jack. Then I fired a seven under par 28 on the first nine and jumped right into the thick of the tournament. After that burst of golf I figured there was nothing I couldn't do and that my first tournament win must be just a lucky break away.

I was in a pretty good mood when I headed for Portland and the next stop. I started out with a first-round 65, still not good enough to lead Nicklaus, who opened with a 64. After that I faded back into the bunch and Nicklaus — despite a two-stroke penalty for slow play — went on to win his second in a row.

This was the first time in my days on the tour that this sort of penalty had been meted out. Many players have been warned for dawdling, but none actually punished. Nicklaus is a thorough, deliberate player, and at Portland the PGA's tournament supervisor Joe Black finally decided that he had become just a shade *too* thorough and deliberate. When Jack had finished his second round with a 67, Black informed him that his score was actually two shots higher than the one he had shot. It came as quite a shock to Jack, of course, and it took a good deal of courage on Black's part. Imagine the second-guessing that would have filled the air, not to mention the newspapers, if Nicklaus, instead of winning the tournament by a stroke, had lost it by that margin.

For me the important thing to come out of the Portland Open was a caddy named Wally Heron. I had seen him at other tournaments and liked his looks — he is fifty-five, gray-haired and always presents a neat, well-pressed exterior — so when he asked to carry my bag I took him on.

Wally Heron is a member of that special breed, the touring caddy, a group that is encountered at practically every tournament on the tour. Some of them are young, some old, some white, some Negro, but they all have in common an intense love of the game of golf. They must have or they wouldn't follow the tour all year round, traveling heaven knows how, sleeping God knows where, and working for a barely adequate income.

Wally Heron carried my bag right through that successful 1962 fall season. He felt that when I won, he won. The relationship between player and caddy is a very close one, especially in a tight tournament, and he had as big a part in the success that was soon to come as I did. Practically all of the touring caddies feel this same identity with the players for whom they work.

The sponsors at each tournament make their own rules about who can caddy and who cannot. As a result the touring caddies are barred at about fifteen of the forty-five tournaments on the schedule each year. Despite this curtailment of job opportunities at least two dozen caddies travel with the tour just about full-time. Wally is pretty typical. So is another caddy named Roy Stone, a colorful-looking character who might be right out of Oliver Twist if it weren't for his Texas accent. Some are tall, like Hagen, who regularly caddies for Doug Ford, Dow Finsterwald and Arnold Palmer; or short, like Burt, a young Scot of about thirty who dresses with the style and color of the players he works for and who often picks up jobs at various tournaments as an assistant caddy master. Only a touring caddy with a Scottish accent could wangle a job like that.

Though some of the touring caddies are heavy drinkers, who find the pro tour a good way to spend very little time working and a lot of time drinking, most of them are out on the tour simply because this is the only kind of life that makes them happy. It has gotten under their skins, just the way playing the tour has gotten under the skin of so many players. Some of them can hardly swing a club and others were once very good players. They suffer with your bad shots and exult with your good ones. They are surprisingly willing to work hard, hour after hour, shagging balls, cleaning your clubs and sometimes even trying to give you tips that will improve your game. Some of them, since they have seen so many great players for so many years, are quite capable of handing out intelligent advice.

Wally Heron's main job when he was caddying for me was not necessarily to tell me which club to use. His main talent was that he knew how to keep me relaxed even when I was getting into a fit of nervousness or anger. He had a way of sensing when this was about to happen, and he knew what to do to snap me out of the mood before it began to ruin my play. Often he would bawl me out for falling asleep on a simple shot. At other times he would tell a joke to relax me, or rub me on the back or bang me on the shoe with the putter just to let me know that he was there and that he knew what was up. Often, when things looked a little tight, the way they got at Las Vegas during the Sahara tournament, or at Orange County where I was about to win my first official title, he would try to explain just how fortunate I was even to be in contention, that I had received good breaks along with the bad and would get more good breaks if I kept working hard. It was an immense comfort to have him there.

A PGA rule specifies that no caddy can work your bag more than two weeks in a row. Since each tournament also has its own regulations, some weeks it becomes pretty difficult to get the one you want. One ploy, if it is an event that insists that the caddies be assigned by the club and by the luck of the draw only, is to tell a hard-luck story to the caddy master. You explain that your touring caddy owes you a great deal of money and that the only way you can settle the debt is to have him caddy for you that week. This approach works one week, but not the next. Often a player will just keep firing the caddy assigned to him until the caddy master in despair gives him the one he has wanted all along. A few caddies have quit on me, for various reasons, but I would never fire one. On the weeks when a player's own particular touring caddy can't work the usual practice is for the player to give him a little money to tide him over until the next week or the next tournament at which he can work. The association becomes almost an adoption.

Their value is worth the effort. One of the great assets these caddies have is that they are completely trustworthy. You can trust them with your money, your golf clubs and even your car. Wally would take my clubs home to clean them, or shellac the woods. He was always utterly dependable. If I told him I would meet him by the practice tee at 8 o'clock the next morning, he would be there, without fail, at 8 o'clock the next morning, even if I didn't get there until 10. The touring caddies are available for running errands. They take clothes to the laundry or dry cleaner, meet your wife at the airport if you have to be somewhere else, drive your car to the next tournament if you have decided to fly.

The life is a hard one because there is not much money in it, and so the caddies come and go. Wally suddenly dropped off the tour during the summer of '63 and returned home to Los Angeles, and his off-tour occupation as a car washer. When I am winning big checks I usually pay my caddy from $150 to $250 a week, but a caddy has to be working a winner's bag to make that kind of money. The caddy I had at the Masters, a fellow named Pokey, who was assigned by the club, got a check for $700. I had won $12,000 that week, however, and Pokey was worth every cent. Generally the rate for a caddy at a PGA tournament is a flat fee of five dollars per round and a dollar an hour for shagging balls. This is pretty nearly rock-bottom wages so most of us, even when we finish out of the money, generally give the caddy $50 or $60 if he was any good at all.

With the development of electric and gasoline golf carts the caddy problem at club after club has become a fairly acute one. Even the members during the course of the year sometimes have a tough time lining up a caddy because fewer kids, not to mention grown men, want to compete with the golf cart. The money simply is not worth it. Then suddenly 150 pros show up for a tournament and all of them need caddies. Most tournament sponsors must train a special group of high school or college age boys to work the tournament. These trainees may try very hard, but the chances are that they are too inexperienced to know much about the golf course you are playing or even much about their jobs. Under these circumstances the value of a touring caddy increases. He may not know the course too well, but he knows everything else. In addition, his wide experience is a shortcut to helping the player size up the course. One exception to this was Julie Boros's caddy in the U.S. Open at Brookline. He wasn't a caddy, he didn't know golf very well and he certainly didn't know the course at all. But he was smart and he worked hard. One day he simply went out and paced off the course so he knew how far it was to the center of each green from just about any point on or off the fairway. It helped in at least a small way to make Julie the new Open champion.

Very often when a player stumbles across a good local caddy at one of the weekly circuit events he will try to persuade him to come on out on the tour and give caddying a whirl for a while. For a young fellow at loose ends it can at least be an educational few months. The player will perhaps draw up a letter of recommendation, give it to this caddy, and the letter can be used as an introduction the first time its owner decides to come out. A Hartford boy, for instance, who has done a good job at the Insurance City Open, may suddenly show up at the Doral Open in Miami, show his letter of introduction to the caddy master and begin working right away, usually for the player who persuaded him to try the tour in the first place.

A number of the touring caddies have complained that the jumps between tournaments have become too long and that the money they earn doesn't justify the hard work and hard traveling they do. I fear that they will soon become extinct as a part of professional tournament society. I certainly hope not. The tour wouldn't be the same without them.

Wally Heron, who had first picked up my bag at Portland,

was still with me a week later in Las Vegas when I got the lucky break that more than wiped out all the bad luck I had ever had on a golf course. The tour was playing in an event called the Sahara Invitational pro-am. With 360 amateurs and 120 pros competing, the tournament, at least for the first two rounds, had to be held on two different courses, the Paradise Valley Country Club and the Las Vegas municipal course. Each professional was scheduled to go 72 holes, but since we were partnered with amateurs for the first 36 the PGA, under a new ruling, declared the tournament to be "unofficial." This meant that money earned in the Sahara would not count on the official money list, it would not entitle the winner to an invitation to play in the Tournament of Champions and would not count in points toward the Ryder Cup team. It was really nothing more than a glorified pro-am, but the field was a strong one and the money you earned that week would be real.

My first round was scheduled at Paradise Valley. I couldn't seem to get myself comfortable when I stood to address the ball and had to work hard just to shoot a 75. I thought, "Well, there's another tournament shot." Several players had already turned in 65's. I went back to my hotel for a nap and to ready myself for the evening of gambling and dancing. It had been a pleasant enough day in spite of my bad golf. I was just a bit incredulous when a friend called me up and said, "Gee, you're lucky. It rained so hard over at Paradise Valley that the first round has been postponed." I thought that this was a very poor joke, but I went downstairs to investigate just the same. The afternoon was still warm with no sign of its having rained. This didn't surprise me. When does it ever rain in Las Vegas? In a moment I found out when. Trooping into the hotel lobby were a group of players so wet and wrinkled they looked as if they'd just climbed out of a swimming pool and not come from a golf course. Yes, it had rained, one of them said, at Paradise Valley. A cloudburst at the course had dumped so much water on just two of the greens that they became unplayable. According to the rules all scores were thus null and void; including a bunch of 65's and my 75.

No golfer could have asked for a stronger omen than that. The next day I got up very early and practiced long and hard prior to my scheduled tee-off time. I worked my way into a nice, comfortable square stance and began hitting the ball well again. In the new first round I scored a 69, followed this with a 67 and then, when the rainout had caused the last two rounds to be played on Sunday, shot the two best scores of the day, a 66 and a 68. I won the tournament by three shots over Don January and six over Billy Casper. It was my first really important victory on the tour. The fact that it was an unofficial tournament, however, still kept me from tasting true, sweet success. But at least it proved that I had the golf game to win a bona fide, official tournament. The question remaining was — as Danny Kaye had put it — did I have the guts? I got the answer three weeks later.

In the two weeks following my victory in the Sahara pro-am event I had come very close in two official PGA events, but had been squeezed out narrowly each time. In the Bakersfield Open I had tied for the lead with Billy Casper after three rounds, but he came in with a very strong 67 on the final day and I finished second by four strokes. At the Ontario, California, Open the next week I led the field with a 135 after two rounds, but reacted badly to the pressure, shot a third-round 74, and eventually finished in a tie for seventh, two shots behind winner Al Geiberger. The experience had been very frustrating. I decided to try at least one more tournament before taking a nice, long vacation. I was playing well, but I was getting kind of pooped. Especially after being in serious contention at so many tournaments in such a short stretch of time.

At the Orange County Open, however, there was absolutely no sign that my golf swing or my nerves were about to collapse. A third-round 64 jumped me into a two-stroke lead over Bob Rosburg and on the last day, when he finished ahead of me with a 67, I managed a shaky par on the last hole to tie him. That sent us into a sudden death play-off. By this time my nerves *were* shot. Here I had this great chance, right in the palm of my hand. But Rosburg was playing well while I was playing badly. Thank goodness Danny Arnold was there. He walked beside me, talking, talking, talking. Under the *Rules of Golf* he was not permitted to give me any advice or information, but he was allowed to keep me calm enough to stay on the course. After I barely toppled in a three-foot putt on the seventy-second hole to tie Rosburg for first place I checked the scoreboard, knew definitely that there was a tie, and rushed over to the first tee where the play-off would start.

The first hole of the Mesa Verde Country Club in Costa Mesa is a par five that doglegs to the right. Rosburg hit two beautiful shots that left him right in front of the green. I hooked my drive, sliced my second shot and so was 40 yards to the right of the green. From there I pitched on three feet from the hole and we both made our birdies.

The second hole is a short par four and the green sits above the fairway blocking off a view of the bottom of the flagstick. Bob played a smooth wedge that flew above our range of vision and onto the green. When the crowd up around the green yelled I judged that he was about two or three feet from the cup. It turned out he was about six feet away. I was very shaky and played a poor wedge shot to the back edge of the green. I was faced with a long downhill putt, but rolled it to within a foot and a half of the hole. This fine approach may have jarred Bob a bit because though his putt for a winning birdie was a simple one, straight uphill, he hit it too softly and it broke wide of the hole to the left.

The third hole was a par three. The green was elevated and the cup was cut into the left side. The proper shot would be a hook that started toward the right side of the green, safely away from danger, and then turned in toward the flag. Bob hit exactly that shot and his ball stopped no more than 10 feet from the hole. I had been having trouble trying to hook the ball so I decided to take a chance, fading the ball out to the left of the green and hoping that it would come back in near the pin. I hit exactly that shot and the ball stopped no more than 10½ feet from the hole.

I was away and it was therefore my turn to putt first. As I got over the ball I suddenly felt certain that I was going to make the putt. I could almost see the exact line to the hole as if the greenskeeper had painted it there. I was equally certain that if I made the putt I would win the play-off. My confidence was supreme and I stroked the ball straight into the hole. Then I stood by the edge of the green, unable to control my fidgeting, and watched while Rosburg's putt hit the back of the cup and bounced out. Bob was inconsolable. Since his last victory, at the Bing Crosby pro-am in January, 1961, he had finished second six times. On three of those occasions he had been defeated in a sudden death play-off. "I guess I'm just a loser," he sighed. Bob, of course, isn't a loser. He has won six tournaments on the tour, including the 1959 PGA championship, and it was of particular significance to me that I had been able to beat a player of his immense abilities.

When Rosburg missed that putt and when I finally came back to earth I was so exhilarated that I think I kissed Danny and shook hands with his wife. The day before, while I was drinking beer and being interviewed in the press room, I had told the sportswriters present that I would order champagne for everyone, not beer, if I was lucky enough to win the tournament. I made good my promise, of course, and have decided it was something I would do henceforth, at every tournament I won. My preference is for Moët, and I'm damned sorry that I have not had the privilege of serving it more often.

Despite the fact that I was pretty well worn-out I decided, since I was riding a hot streak, to stay with the tour a few weeks longer. The two players who compile the best performance figures on the fall and winter schedules earn Masters invitations. I certainly did not want to miss out on that. I was also piling up a great many Ryder Cup points and, if I could continue to play well, might even accumulate enough through the 1963 PGA tournament, when the team was chosen, to be named. So I doggedly played on. At the Mobile Open in November I won again. During the third round I was paired with Johnny Pott and Gay Brewer, each of whom had done well in Mobile previously, Gay having won it the year before, and I was very gratified to hear them say how well they thought I was playing. Coming down the eighteenth fairway on the final day I had an eight-shot lead and for the first time felt I could relax in a golf tournament. The gallery was shouting at me, asking if I thought my lead was safe. I shouted back, yes, I thought it was, if I was careful on the last hole. I bogeyed it to beat Doug Sanders by seven shots.

From Mobile I went on to Mexico City and successfully defended my Mexican Open title. Then I took the last month of the year off. I had done enough, I thought. My total earnings had come to $48,000. I had drawn even with sponsor Crocker, I had finally won my first official tournament and I could look forward to playing in my first Masters. I even had enough money left over to buy my mother a mink coat. It was a very happy Christmas for the Lema family in Oakland. I was eager to start out the next year and prove that my play during the autumn of 1962 had not been a fluke.

# 14 / High stakes and practice rounds

G OLF tournaments are exciting, but a smart spectator can have quite a bit of fun taking a close look at the golf that is played before the tournament even begins. Most fans must think that a pre-tournament practice round is nothing more than that, a practice round. The primary purpose is, of course, to furnish a look at the golf course and keep the swing grooved, but there is a good deal more than that involved.

First of all, while the partners we play with in the tournament are assigned, in practice we play with whom we darn please, namely our close friends. This, plus the fact that we *are* practicing, makes for an atmosphere that is as relaxed as a Sunday picnic.

Secondly, despite the friendship, there is always a little money riding on every practice round match. Doug Ford has said that he never likes to play *any* round of golf unless it is for at least $10 or $20. If he is not playing for something more vital than just learning about the golf course he finds himself getting careless and sloppy. This is a sloppiness that can easily carry over into the tournament itself. Some of the players are only competing for a two-dollar Nassau — meaning a bet of two dollars on the first nine, two dollars on the second nine, and two dollars on the entire 18 — during practice. Others like Al Besselink, who is no longer on the tour, or Doug Sanders, who is still very much on the tour, will play for considerably more, possibly as high as $500 or $1000 for the match.

The competition will take several forms. Two players will play against each other in a singles match, two teams will play a best ball match against each other, or a combination of the two will be going on simultaneously. Let's say that Ken Venturi, Tommy Jacobs, Johnny Pott and myself are playing together. Ken and I may be paired against the best ball of the other two while at the same time I am playing a singles match against Pott and Jacobs is playing a singles match against Ken. We may be playing for a flat fee on the medal score for 18 holes or we may be playing a Nassau, which is a hole-by-hole match play competition, and the most commonly used form.

Whatever the teams or the form of the contest these competitions usually have one thing in common, something that may seem peculiar to many observers. This is the fact that there is almost never any handicapping. You may often see, therefore, a player who has won a few tournaments and ranks in the top five of the money list playing against a nonentity who has never even won a pro-am and is lucky to be in the top fifty on the official money list. Not taking strokes from another player becomes a question of pride out here on the tour. Each player is a professional who thinks himself capable of producing a good round of golf every day and therefore capable of beating any one, Arnold Palmer included. I have seen Sam Snead working very hard to win a practice round match against a player most spectators may never have heard of. Often this discrepancy is reduced by a fair team arrangement, but not always. Most players, however, will avoid a big money match with a fellow pro who happens to be on a hot streak, or simply stop gambling with a player they have never been able to beat in a head-to-head match.

It is not a particularly good idea to get too wrapped up in a practice round match by betting a lot of money on it. The most I have ever risked is a straight $200 for 18 holes. Prior to the Hot Springs, Arkansas, Open in 1958 I got involved in a high-betting practice round with the tour's two prize hustlers, Besselink and Sanders. We played nine holes the first day and I lost $50 to each of them. The next day we upped the ante to $100 and I took one bet from Bessie, but lost the other. I was pretty green to be going in for this sort of thing and, since I stood to lose $200, was lucky to break even.

One objection to over-betting is that a player should not be giving his all in a practice round. He should be learning something about the course and experimenting with certain shots he may want to use when the tournament bell rings. I have explained Jerry Barber's habit of playing, when he first came out on the tour, for high stakes with the top players just to get a firsthand look at their techniques. Quite a few players operate on the same theory, but I find I can learn fully as much just by strolling out on the course now and then to follow some of the hot players for a few holes. Therefore in my practice rounds I prefer to play with my friends, some of whom *are* top players, and never for more than about a five-dollar Nassau. Even then you may find yourself engaged in a match that has snowballed financially.

Phil Rodgers and I team together frequently in two-dollar best ball Nassau matches and we have been in a couple that involved a payoff about as close to the original bet as church bingo is to the casino at the Desert Inn. Prior to the 1962 San Francisco Open we took on Dick Whetzle and Rex Baxter, a couple of young Texas pros who hardly had a tournament record to match ours, but apparently had plenty of confidence. It was for two dollars a side and two dollars for the match. They fell behind and pressed us a couple of times, meaning that every time they got two holes down they were allowed to start a new bet on the remaining holes. By the sixteenth tee Phil and I were a modest $12 each ahead. At that point they exercised an option and so we played the sixteenth for double or nothing. Phil birdied the hole and put us $24 ahead. We played the seventeenth for a straight $10 and I won that for us with a birdie that jumped us $34 in front. Going to the last hole Whetzle and Baxter figured we couldn't have any more birdies in us so they splurged and we played the last hole for double what we had already won. I whipped in another birdie to beat them and Phil and I had cleared over $100 each on something that had started as a two-dollar Nassau.

A couple of years ago Phil and I had a fairly profitable practice round match in Portland against Dan Sikes, the Florida attorney, and young Tommy Aaron. Again the match was a two-dollar Nassau. I birdied the first hole, Phil birdied the second, and then I birdied the third, fourth, fifth, sixth and seventh right in a row. To put the icing on this cake Phil threw in a birdie on the eighth hole. Sikes, who is tall and lanky and has a very strong Florida accent, kept mumbling and moaning and shaking his head, but he and Aaron kept pressing and pressing and pressing, and falling further and further into the hole. Phil and I slowed down a little on the back nine, but not much. Despite the fact that Sikes scored a birdie on the last hole that saved him and Tommy a big bundle, we still came out $50 ahead.

A final point that often makes a practice round well worth a spectator's time and energy is the good-natured verbal needling that goes on. In a practice round nothing is sacred. We like to kid each other about the size of our bellies or our bankrolls, the loop at the top of a backswing or the apple that comes up in an opponent's throat when he needs to hole a tricky downhill putt to win a press. Despite the fact that substantial sums of money will sometimes ride along on the result of a practice round it is a time when the touring pro can really have some fun playing golf. The fun ends when the grim business of the tournament begins.

# 15 / The Masters: fun at the summit

THERE are many examples of players on the pro tour who have reached the crest of stardom one year only to fade gently into obscurity the next. These fade-outs do not necessarily take the form of the severe slumps that have hit Mike Souchak or Ken Venturi. More often it starts when a player suddenly shows a great deal of promise and it is assumed that he will continue to grow and succeed as a golfer in the years immediately following his first splurge. When he does not — and the chances are at least fifty–fifty that he will not — a vacuum is created in the place he was slated to fill. He wins a tournament every now and then, but never a major one. He misses the cut and the money quite a bit and his name fades from the headlines as quickly as it originally burst into print. Sometimes these players begin to make their mark again years later. Sometimes they never do. They remain good, average-playing pros, but often nothing more.

Look first at the record of Bobby Nichols. In 1962 Bobby was only twenty-six, but he won two tournaments, finished ninth on the money list with a total of $34,312. He also came within a few holes of winning the U.S. Open, where he finally tied for third with Phil Rodgers, two shots behind Nicklaus and Palmer. Nichols, a Texan who had been so severely injured in a high school auto accident that he was unconscious for thirteen days, looked like one of the golfers to beat in 1963 because he would be a year older and a year more experienced. Well, Nichols is still a fine young man and a very fine golfer, but somehow in 1963 the promise was not quite fulfilled. He won a tournament at the tail end of the year, but slipped to tenth on the money list, earning $1000 less than he had the year before.

Phil Rodgers makes an even more dramatic point. If Jack Nicklaus had not joined the tour at virtually the same time Phil would have been the odds-on choice as golf's rookie of the year in 1962. He started his first full year on the tour by winning the Los Angeles Open with a fantastic final round of 62. He won the Tucson Open, finished third in the British Open, led the U.S. Open with six holes to play before falling back into a tie with Nichols, and finished eleventh on the money list. Phil is still a fine fellow and a very fine golfer, but what happened to him in 1963? Nothing too terrible. He won the Texas Open and tied for first in the British Open before losing a play-off to left-hander Bob Charles. But aside from these two brief eruptions nothing was heard from Phil Rodgers. His overall earnings tumbled by $10,000 and he plunged all the way down to twenty-ninth on the official earnings list.

In 1963 Raymond Floyd, Mason Rudolph, Tommy Aaron, Bob Charles and Jack Rule blossomed almost as brightly as Nichols and Rodgers did the year before. At the end of the year there seemed to be little question that their careers were headed for a glorious future. But what will happen to them in 1964? I do not mean to say that none of the six players I have mentioned above will ever make it as big stars. There is a good chance that more than one of them will do so. The harsh fact of the pro tour is, however, that one brilliant year does not guarantee a future of crowded trophy cases and bulging bank accounts.

With facts like this in mind you can imagine that I faced the 1963 season with a certain amount of apprehension. I felt reasonably sure that it was my five years of hard experience on the tour and my more mature attitude toward competitive golf that had suddenly made me a winner in the fall of 1962. But I could not be *sure* until I saw what happened in 1963. At the outset of the year I felt that I *had* to keep winning to prove myself. Strange to say it was not a win at all, but a second-place finish — in the first Masters Championship I had ever played in — that gave me the confidence to make the year a truly successful one.

The winter tour, in fact, was marked by my second-place finishes. At San Diego, in the second week of the season, Gary Player sank a 20-foot putt for a par on the very last hole of the tournament to beat me by a stroke. I was sitting in the press room at the time listening to a broadcast of the tournament on the radio. With Gary needing to get down a 20-footer to beat me I was getting myself ready for the sudden death play-off I felt confident would go my way. Two seconds later I was on my way to Pebble Beach instead. I continued to play well and pick up checks at the Bing Crosby, the San Francisco Open, at Palm Springs and at Phoenix. I had a good chance to win at New Orleans, but finally tied for second with Bob Rosburg, two shots behind winner Bo Wininger. I had a good chance to win the Doral Open in Miami despite an opening-round 75, but finished third by three shots behind winner Dan Sikes and runner-up Sam Snead. This was my final tournament before the Masters. All these close finishes without a victory had been very frustrating, but I felt my first win was coming up soon. I was also fourth on the money list, thanks to some good checks, with a total of $14,831 as the tour came into Augusta, Georgia. Ahead of me were golf's so-called Big Three: Player, who led with a total of $23,502, Palmer, who had already won three tournaments and $23,225, and burly Jack Nicklaus, pretty far behind the other two with $16,715.

In addition to the money I won I also found that I had reached a high if not exalted station on the tour. Now tournament sponsors would come after me, trying to make sure that I would be playing in their tournament. All of a sudden people were doing favors for me: making plane and hotel reservations, meeting me at the airport when I arrived in town, seeing to it that a new car was at my disposal while I was there. This is standard treatment for the top players on the pro tour. If we felt so inclined many of us would never have to lift a finger to travel the whole circuit. We are wined, dined, praised, chauffeured, flattered, partied, toasted, served, adored, caressed, coddled, pampered and spoiled. I am impressed by the fact that even once-negligent locker room attendants suddenly have a big, bright smile, and a big, bright, clean new locker for me every time I check in at a club.

It was just around the time of the Masters that I began to receive quite a bit of publicity in various national golfing and sporting publications. I can't say that I really liked any of it at first. *Golf Digest,* a monthly magazine that only a golfer could love, painted me as the lover-boy of the tour, a playboy constantly surrounded by beautiful babes. *Sports Illustrated* suggested in a feature article that I was nothing but a playboy who threw rousing champagne parties at which my guests drove golf balls out of hotel windows. Somehow, this was not the image of myself that I had created in my own mind. Crocker had insisted I travel the tour first class as part of our arrangement and I had done so. There had been women, champagne and a few parties, to be sure, but nothing extravagant and seldom in the midst of a tournament. Therefore the picture of me as Playboy Tony on the Tour was a little alarming. At first, and I guess most people in the public eye will agree with me, stories about oneself are always something of a shock. Few people ever recognize themselves in a story written by another. It takes getting used to but I began to get used to it. Not because I will ever be convinced that I am a fanatical party lover, but because I began to realize that national acclaim is what I must have had in mind away back in those days at Elko when I was winning tournaments against Walt Harrison and Cliff Whittle, but dreaming about beating Ben Hogan and Sam Snead. Why fight it?

National publicity and some solid, if runner-up performances had placed me among the favorites as the eighty-five or so players invited to play in the Masters began to collect in Augusta during early April. Being one of the favorites is a role that no one really enjoys except, of course, that it usually means you are playing pretty good golf. To someone unaccustomed to it, like myself, it creates the sensation of being out in front where everyone can take a shot at you. It builds up a psychological burden just at the moment when you are doing your best to reduce the pressure. One trick I resort to that probably doesn't do any good at all, but at least makes me *feel* good, is to tell any reporter interested that I have shot abnormally high practice round scores. During my first few trips around the Augusta National course I would intentionally score high on a couple of holes, without its affecting my overall play, if I thought a sportswriter might be looking on. Then later, if anyone from the press asked me what I had shot in a practice round, I would say, "A bunch over par."

While everyone playing at Augusta feels the pressure, the first thing I discovered as I began to learn my way around is that the Masters is fun. The stakes are high, of course, the pressure to win is great, but the pleasure of playing in a tournament on the Augusta National is so acute that it almost completely wipes out the pain of nervous tension. The Masters is a tournament one looks forward to expectantly, eagerly, with the knowledge that win or lose you are going to enjoy yourself.

The first time that real inside knowledge of this tournament ever reached down into my rather limited experience was in 1956 when Ken Venturi, then an amateur, almost won it. Ken's performance caused quite a stir around his hometown of San Francisco, so even Tony Lema, who knew Venturi only by reputation, got the word that the Masters was a pretty big deal. Two months later, when I had amazingly qualified to play in the U.S. Open, and then, even more incredibly, made the 36-hole cutoff, I heard about the Masters again. I was paired the last day with a young pro from Georgia named Walker Inman, Jr. His concern at the time was not to win the U.S. Open, which he had very little chance to do after shooting a 77 and a 72 for the first two rounds, but to qualify for the Masters the following year. To do so he had to finish in the top sixteen at Rochester. This was the first time I got any inkling of the fact that the Masters is strictly an invitational tournament. The golfers who play there are invited because of their record in past competition. There are many ways a man can qualify but basically it is limited to British Open, U.S. Open, British Amateur, U.S. Amateur, and PGA champions of the preceding ten years; all former Master champions, the low twenty-four at the most recent U.S. Open, the low eight at the most recent PGA and U.S. Amateur Championships, the low twenty-four from the Masters of the year before and all recent Ryder and Walker Cup players. In addition some players are invited off their showing on the pro tour, some are elected by past U.S. Open, Masters and Amateur champions, and a big list of talented foreign players are invited.

Inman, who unfortunately failed to qualify for the Masters that day, also described to me the vast charm of the golf course itself, how well run the tournament was and what a terrific deal in general it was to play there. I was impressed, of course, but playing in the Masters was about as far from my mind at that time as reenlisting in the U.S. Marines. It seemed like a faraway Shangri-la, closed to the likes of a greenhorn assistant pro like Tony Lema. That type would never make it to Augusta and wasn't even going to try.

After I had gone on the tournament circuit I began, of course, to hear a great deal about this glorious event. Naturally, I watched it on television each year. CBS has always done a superb job of televising the Masters and the Masters has returned the compliment by seldom putting on a dull tournament. In 1957 Doug Ford holed out of a trap in front of the eighteenth green for a 66 that won the tournament and it happened too early for the cameras to catch. But in 1958 they caught Ford and Fred Hawkins missing short putts on the eighteenth that would have tied Palmer; in 1959 they showed millions of viewers Art Wall completing his winning finish of five birdies on the last six holes; in 1960, a sad year for San Franciscans, the camera recorded Palmer's miraculous birdie-birdie finish that beat Venturi by a stroke; in 1961 Palmer came on screen at the eighteenth hole needing only a par to win the tournament, then hit into a trap and double-bogeyed the hole to finish second and give an astonished Gary Player, who was also on camera watching Arnold on camera, his victory; then in 1962 the cameras recorded the finishes

[ 197 ]

that put Player, Palmer and Finsterwald into a three-way tie, and a play-off that Palmer subsequently won.

Through the years I had been obliged to watch all these tournaments on a TV screen, because I had never done anything that earned me the right to play there. But finally, on the basis of my performance on the fall tour of 1962, I earned an invitation. Everything about the place more than justified the thrill I got from having made it to Augusta National at last.

From the moment I turned off the main highway and into the long, magnolia-lined driveway that leads to the white Georgian colonial clubhouse, I felt that I was in the center of old-world Southern plantation life. The main building looks like a tobacco baron's mansion and when a player arrives he is treated like an honored guest, or a visiting diplomat. A doorman seized my clubs and rushed them off to the caddy house. I stepped inside the door, registered at the front desk and was led upstairs to my locker. It was located smack under four pictures of Bob Jones, the club's president, sinking the four winning putts that brought him the Grand Slam of Golf in 1930. Around the clubhouse were framed photographs of past Masters winners: Horton Smith, Gene Sarazen, Craig Wood, Byron Nelson, Snead, Hogan, Palmer, and all the others. Around the clubhouse were also these people in person and many others; U.S. Open Amateur and PGA champions of long ago; Freddie McLeod who won the Open in 1908, Jock Hutchison who won the British Open in 1921, and others. The atmosphere gave me a tingly feeling in the guts because it seemed as if a picture history book of golf had been suddenly brought to life.

Nor was my first look at the golf course any less exciting. In fact, it is the finest course I have ever seen or played on.

## The Masters: fun at the summit

The tournament and the course have been in existence for almost thirty years and the tournament committee, which is run by Jones himself and New York banker Cliff Roberts, have accumulated that much experience in grooming the course and putting on their show. The fairways are lush and wide. Every hole is unique and carefully planned as to where the tee shot might be placed, or where the cup might be cut into the green. When you get out on the course you feel you just can't get enough of it. I wanted to lie down and roll around on it it looked so beautiful. The Masters is played in April each year, and the dogwood, azalea and other shrubbery are in full bloom. The course is a white, red, purple, pink and green paradise.

The Venturis, Ken and his wife Connie, had invited me and Bo Wininger to share the three-bedroom house they had rented near the course for $300. This made it very convenient for Ken and me to play our practice rounds together — we were joined by Byron Nelson — and it was these sessions that made it possible for me to do as well at Augusta as I did. As we played, Ken and Byron chatted about shots they had hit in past tournaments, where the pins were likely to be placed and what to do on certain holes if the wind was blowing. I kept my eyes and ears open and even though they would be playing against me in the tournament, they answered in accurate detail every question I asked. I learned, for instance, that the two shortest par four holes on the course, the 355-yard third and the 365-yard seventh, could be the most difficult. When the tournament started I resolved to play my second shots right into the middle of the green and settle for pars on these holes. I also learned that though the fairways are exceptionally wide (Augusta has a total of 70 acres of fairway, compared to the standard of about 35 acres) this was a subtle

deception. In order to have anything but an extremely difficult approach shot into each green the tee shot must be very
carefully placed as well as hit pretty far. As Jones has said:
"Augusta is not a difficult course for the weekend amateur
who is frankly seeking bogeys. But for the player who wants
nothing but pars and birdies it can be an extremely difficult
test."

That is what I learned in my practice rounds. That you
have to be a very gutsy player to score well and win at Augusta. You have to be playing well, but you also have to cut
the corners and get as near to the green off the tee as you can.
If you play safe you have so many long approach shots and
so many long putts that you will have very little chance of
winning.

After my last practice round I asked Nelson what he
thought of my swing and how he thought I was playing. He
stopped, took a long look at me and said, "I've watched your
swing for three days now. I've observed you pretty carefully
and I cannot see a thing wrong. I think you're swinging and
hitting the ball beautifully." This gave me so much confidence
and made me feel so good I felt like dancing a jig on the
clubhouse veranda. I could hardly wait for the tournament
to start.

When I got on the first tee the next day I was pretty tense.
I was actually wondering if I would be able to even get the
ball off the tee and down the fairway. So I teed my ball up,
stepped back from it for a moment and took a deep breath,
then stepped up and just hit it as hard as I could. When I
looked up I could see the ball soaring away, way out, right
down the middle. I had hit the drive about 300 yards, but I
pulled a 9-iron approach into the trap on the left of the green.
The ball was buried in the sand, but I blasted it out to about
10 feet from the hole and then sank the putt for a par. I felt

I was off and running. Actually I was just a little tense during the whole round and couldn't drive the ball as well as I wanted, but I was pleased with my 74. I had been paired with Tommy Bolt, and while he has a reputation as a hot-tempered, explosive player, playing with Tommy is something I actually enjoy. Tommy responds to compliments as brightly as most people do. So whenever I am with him I always point out to him what a great player he is, how great he is playing that day or how many great shots he is hitting. Tommy knows I am laying it on pretty thick, but nothing I say isn't based on fact. It just puts us both in a good mood and the round becomes a distinct pleasure.

During the second round I was paired with Snead and again my confidence was given a big boost. I shot a 69 to Snead's 73, and actually hit some shots that prompted Snead to say "Nice shot." Sam doesn't usually smile too much or say too much during a round. It is almost as if he were alone on the course with his caddy and the gallery. I figured if I had reached the point where Sam Snead was commenting on my good play then I must be playing super golf. This put me into contention and when I shot a 74 during the wet, cold and rainy third round I maintained my position. I started the final round at 217, in fifth place and three shots back of Jack Nicklaus.

The feeling I had before the round started is something I can never forget. I was upstairs in the clubhouse looking at the pairing sheet posted on the bulletin board and checking the comparative scores. Dan Sikes came up the stairs and stood next to me, also studying the list. "Tony," he said in his Florida drawl, "you just might be able to win this thing."

"Attorney," I said, "I feel so charged up I could just walk out the door to the porch over there, walk right through the railing and float straight to the first tee."

That's the way I felt the entire afternoon. I thought that if I could play a steady front nine I would be in a very good position to win. I played it in 35, one under par and when I checked the huge scoreboard as I walked to the tenth tee I could see that I had gained a stroke on Nicklaus. On the tenth hole I hit a strong drive down the left side and then a 5-iron shot to 12 feet from the hole. The putt was a good one, but it whirled around the edge of the hole and stayed out. On the eleventh hole my approach shot was hit well, but I had used the wrong club — a 5-iron instead of a 4-iron, and though I reached the green I was about 100 feet short of the hole. I three-putted for a bogey. Nicklaus was playing two groups in back of me with Julius Boros. Gary Player and Sam Snead were up in front of me and the tournament had now been distilled down to the five of us in contention. Then suddenly up ahead of me Snead and Player started to make birdies and so I fell not only back of Jack, but a couple of shots behind Snead and Player as well.

The twelfth hole is a par three where the hazards are a pond in front of the green and a swirly wind that is impossible to outguess. Many a Masters has been lost on this hole. I hit a wonderful shot here and left myself with a putt of no more than eight feet, a putt I desperately needed to stay in the contest. When the putt just missed I could control my temper no longer. As I tapped my second putt into the hole and pulled out the ball I barked out a stream of the filthiest language I had used since mustering out of the Marines in 1955. When I straightened up I noticed my playing partner, a Formosan named Chen Ching-Po, who was also having his troubles in the final round, looking at me in a funny way. I walked over to him and apologized for using such vile language in front of a visitor to my country. He smiled and then said in very broken English: "Is all right. If I knew those words I would use them myself." That made me feel good again and I hit two good shots on the thirteenth hole and birdied it. This put me back to even par in the tournament and in contention once again.

As I played through the fourteenth, fifteenth and sixteenth holes in par the tournament was changing rapidly all around me. Snead and Player inexplicably collapsed on the last few holes; Sam bogeyed the sixteenth and eighteenth, Gary the seventeenth and eighteenth. Now I only needed pars on the last two holes to tie Snead. If I birdied one of them I might even win. I made par on the seventeenth, but by then Nicklaus had birdied the sixteenth so I was two shots back of him as I stood on the eighteenth tee.

The finishing hole at Augusta is an extremely tough par four of 420 yards. It is uphill and doglegs sharply around a group of tall, thick-trunked pine trees on the right. The green is fairly narrow and rises to the back through three distinct plateaus. It is trapped on the right and on the front, and falls off sharply into the TV towers on the left. It is a helluva hole to have to make a birdie three on, but I knew I had absolutely no chance to win the tournament if I didn't. If I did so and Nicklaus, behind me, made a bogey on one of the last two holes — certainly a possibility — I might tie or even beat him. I hit a fine drive past the corner and was about a 4-iron distance from the green.

At this stage I was very nervous and tense, just as anyone might be, but it was an almost enjoyable kind of tension, a charged-up feeling that anything is possible, which focuses your mind down so hard on the shots you have to hit that you are able to shut out everything else. It is something that you learn through experience. You realize that you have a golf club in your hand and that you have a shot to hit. The ball is just sitting there, nobody has stepped on it or is trying to

keep you from hitting it. You just go ahead and do the best
you can without thinking of the consequences of a bad shot
or a good shot. At this moment I know how it feels to Arnold
Palmer when he is pumping himself up emotionally to get set
for one of his fantastic clutch shots. The pin was in the middle terrace of the green, toward the right side. I knew if I
landed the ball on the right side of the green it would kick in
toward the hole. This meant flirting with the trap on the right
side of the green, but I wasn't thinking about the trap. I had
a chance to win the tournament, I was passing this way and
who knows when I would ever be so close again, so I was
just going to take a good, long smell of the flowers. I hit a
very firm 4-iron that struck just off the right side and kicked
up and onto the green, about 22 feet above the hole. Chen
had missed the green so he chipped up stiff to the hole and
putted out for his par.

The scoreboard towering over the eighteenth green showed
that Snead and Player had finished with 288 and 289 respectively, and that only Nicklaus and Boros were out on
the course. I took off my glove, Pokey my caddy and I lined
up the putt, I tossed away my cigarette and got over the
ball. The putt had to slide downhill and break two ways. I
had to start it about six or eight inches to the left of the hole
figuring that it would then break about four or five inches to
the right before turning straight at the hole once again. When
I hit the ball I knew it had a chance. It started out to the
left then swung toward the right just as we had figured it
would. It held that line for a few moments then gradually
swung back to the left again and headed straight for the target. When the ball turned in toward the hole I just knew it
was going to go in and I started to jump. In it went and the
exhilaration and relief I felt were immeasurable. It was like
an explosion inside me. The experience left me pretty wrung

out inside, however, and jumpy. After I signed my card three or four uniformed Burns detectives led me through the crowd and back into Cliff Roberts's private office in the clubhouse, the same room in which Venturi and Player had sat in 1960 and '61, watching Palmer first win the tournament and a year later blow it.

There in Roberts's office were Roberts himself, Bob Jones, whom I was now meeting for the first time, Arnold Palmer and Labron Harris, who was likely to be the low amateur in the Masters. A TV set and TV cameras were also present. Arnie looked pretty glum, but he congratulated me warmly on my fine playing and we all sat down with drinks and watched the set. We saw Nicklaus play the eighteenth, saw his second shot come up too strongly and stop about 40 feet above the hole. At that moment I thought that his downhill putt was so tough that he would surely three-putt the green and put us into a play-off the following day. I was extremely tense at this moment, but I realized — or tried to convince myself — that there was absolutely nothing I could do about it either way. I just had to sit and watch him win the Masters or watch him tie with me. I told myself not to expect anything. His first putt rolled four feet past the hole and when I saw his second putt I thought that it couldn't go in. How it did I will never know. I guess he just had the guts to hit it hard enough. When it dived from sight into the hole so did all my emotions and all my hopes. I felt exactly like a soggy washcloth ready to be wrung out and hung up. I felt I would never have the strength to rise from the chair I was sitting in. There was a lot of incoherent talk and finally Jack came in on Cloud Nine and we all congratulaed him. On my way out to the presentation ceremony Ken Venturi came over and grabbed me and we stepped into a side room to have a short talk. There were tears in Ken's eyes and tears in mine and we staggered around the room like two blind people, trying to regain our composure. Now we both knew what it was to come so close to winning this great tournament and then have it plucked right out of our pocket. We both knew so well how the other had felt. We shook hands and vowed that, of course, we would both be back and one day one of us would win this tournament.

Cliff Roberts hosted a dinner at the club that night. Jack and Barbara Nicklaus were there, Arnold and Winnie, Gary Player and his wife Vivienne, Bill and Shirley Casper and Charlie Coe, a fine amateur player and also a member of the Augusta National. We toasted each other and after dinner Arnold took me aside. He told me how well I had played in my first Masters. He wanted to be considered a real friend of mine, something that particularly warmed me, and told me not to be disappointed about finishing second. How could I? Once the shock had worn off I realized how well I must have played to be the runner-up, only a stroke back of a truly magnificent player like Nicklaus, and how tournament-tough I had become, being able to survive the terrific pressure of those closing holes and finish with a birdie on the last one.

In the weeks to follow I realized how much the Masters had done for me. Perhaps 20,000,000 people had watched the finish on television and I wondered how many other Tony Lemas there were looking at a TV set instead of being on the scene as they surely would be in a few years. From then on I was dogged by reporters and considered a strong favorite at every tournament I played in. I took on a business manager, Fred Corcoran, the bustling Bostonian who had done so much to put the pro tour on its feet during the 1930's. Thanks in part to him business opportunities began to spring up like gushing oil wells, and the confidence I had now gained swept me right through to the end of the year.

# 16 / *Day with a touring pro*

THE telephone rings, I wake from a dreamless sleep and force open my eyes. "Good morning, Mr. Lema," it says. "Six o'clock."

Thus a typical day in the life of a touring pro begins. Exactly like 180 million other Americans he gets up in the morning. Exactly like millions of traveling salesmen he has breakfast in the motel coffee shop. Exactly like 10,000,000 weekend duffers he gets out to the golf course about an hour before his turn to play comes up. He plays his little round of golf in virtual solitude, afterward catches a quick beer in the bar with a couple of the other early birds, then hitches a ride to his motel with a friend or in a tournament courtesy car. Back in his room he suspends himself in a hot tub to let the bogeys and the double-bogeys soak out of his system. His bath is usually followed by a nap, then dinner with a fellow player and maybe a gin or poker game. This exciting day is topped off by a late movie on television and then lights out and sleep.

That, with minor variations, was Tony Lema *circa* 1959, a nonentity then, just a slightly higher class entity today. After five years of hard work I finally reached the point at which my starting times are usually scheduled at a more humane hour and I can sleep a little later in the morning. If I am

having a lucky week and am up among the leaders, I may not
have to play until early in the afternoon.

Let's say I am due to tee off at 1:30 P.M., in which case I
instruct the switchboard operator to ring my room at 9 o'clock.
This will give me plenty of time to do the many things I have
to do before tee time. Some players live in constant fear that
the operator is never going to call. They tell horror stories
about the call that never came one morning, how they overslept and were disqualified for being late on the first tee. The
result is that, even if they don't have to be up until the middle
of the morning, they wake up at 6 o'clock and lie there staring
at the ceiling too terror-stricken to go back to sleep. These
guys ought to carry alarm clocks, but then I guess one morning the alarm wouldn't ring and then where would they be.

I have many psychological quirks but that, thank God, is
not one of them. When wake-up call comes through, my wife
Betty rolls over to catch a few more minutes of sleep and I
light up a cigarette to get me through the shock of having to
face the day. I wait, collecting my thoughts, knowing that the
telephone is going to ring again. This time it will be Fred
Corcoran, my business manager. Fred rings shortly after 9
o'clock. He is short and round and sometimes jolly, but he
also tends to be overanxious about things. Fred wants to
know how I feel, how I played the day before and how I will
play today. Maybe from my answers he gets an idea of my
mood and what items of business it is safe to discuss now,
what items to hold for tomorrow. Then we talk business: a
bid for our endorsement from the manufacturer of a practice
club that clicks when you swing it correctly (no); the offer
of a tie-in with a high-quality, well-known clothing manufacturer (yes); an invitation to play on a filmed TV golf match
(yes, I'll call the producer). Our telephone discussion lasts

twenty minutes. I hang up, light another cigarette and order breakfast for two from room service, usually a substantial one for myself because I may not be eating again until dinner time. Betty is still asleep, but I get up, take a long, hot shower and a leisurely shave. I do everything as slowly as possible now because when I hit the golf course it will be rush, rush, rush; newspaper interviews to give, autographs to sign, telephone calls to return, mail to read. After shaving I dress in the clothes I will be wearing on the golf course, breakfast arrives, Betty wakes up, and we eat. This isn't exactly plush eating, but it's cozy.

When breakfast is over I put the tray outside in the hall and then gulp down a vitamin pill. Just about everyone on the tour is a vitamin pill bug. We gobble them up like turkeys turned loose in a bin of corn. Half the time we don't even know what kind of vitamin it is we are swallowing, but we have complete faith that it will balance our diets, keep our hair from falling out, make us feel fit all day long and add 10 yards to our tee shots.

While Betty is getting dressed I sprawl out on the unmade bed and scribble off a few business and personal letters. I receive about twenty-five to fifty a week that require an answer. Then I go to work again on the phone. This batch of outgoing calls is to future tournament sponsors who want my commitment, the TV producer who wants me on his golf show (I'm sorry to say this type of call is not one I have to make very often), or to the golf equipment company back in San Francisco that makes the line of clubs that carry my name and of which I am one-third owner. During this call I order a new set of clubs for myself and place orders from local pros whom I have persuaded to stock my clubs in their pro shops.

All my outgoing telephone calls, if I think I can get away with it, are made collect.

By this time it is almost 11 o'clock, Betty is dressed and I have smoked at least half a pack of cigarettes. It is also time to leave for the course. This may seem early, but I know from experience (at least when I am playing well and winning a tournament every once in a while) that I must allow comfortably over two hours between the time I park my car at the club and the time the official PGA starter calls my name and I step out on the first tee. Outside is a Buick Riviera. The presence of this gleaming vehicle is part and parcel of the finest car deal the tour has ever had. Buick has set up an arrangement with about a dozen top players which calls for Buick to supply the car and the player simply to drive it. In addition, Buick gives us a late model for use back home. When we are out on the tour a new car will be delivered either to the airport or to the motel. What we get out of this deal is pretty obvious, what they get out of it is a little less so. Undoubtedly, they think that the promotion value of having a bunch of golfers drive around in Buicks is worth the trouble and expense it puts them to. Anyway, Betty and I climb into our shiny, brand-new Buick-for-a-week and cruise out to the course. En route I always maintain that she isn't dressed warmly enough and she maintains just as stoutly that she is.

Once we have parked at the club it takes another fifteen or twenty minutes to get to my first destination — the pro shop and the touring golfer's mailbox. It is usually located in a nice safe place, easily accessible to the public. The walk is a slow one because a great many well-wishers are on hand who want to say hello. There are a forest of autograph books to sign and possibly a couple of newspapermen to talk to as I move along. All this chitchat is time consuming, but I want to give each person the time and consideration his thoughtfulness deserves.

Getting mail on the tour does not resemble mail call in the Marines. There is no mad stampede on the tour. In the Marines I was restless and in a barren, foreign land. Any place in the U.S., however, is home to me and mail is not something I look forward to eagerly as a break in the loneliness. On the tour when your name is in the public eye, it is hard to be lonely. I sort through the batch of stuff in the mailbox cubby hole marked L and separate out anything that is addressed to me. There is usually a packet of letters sent on by my mother from San Leandro. It contains more bills than I can afford to pay, a check from a TV golf show I appeared on, or the bonus check every player receives from the various companies he is tied in with when he wins a tournament. In the collection also is a stack of telegrams. If I have just won a tournament, which happens at least once a year, I receive about fifty congratulatory messages the following week. If I have just shot a good round then there will be an additional ten or twelve wires applauding this remarkable feat. I guess most players just tuck this stuff away in their lockers until they have time to look at it. Not me. I'm like the curious cat and have to sit right down and read everything immediately. This takes another twenty minutes.

While I am changing into my golf shoes in the locker room a couple of newspapermen stop by. One just to say hello or to sound out what my choking threshhold may be. The other is doing a personality column and he will need ten or fifteen minutes of my time. I try to make the interview lively, witty, sincere, hilarious, sentimental, dramatic, colorful and spontaneous, but it is pretty hard to do. After all, I have only answered the same questions one million times already.

The trip from the locker room to the practice tee, the next stop in my crowded program, is also a slow one. More greetings, more autographs. I look for Betty, but she is probably inside the clubhouse having a cup of coffee with one of the other wives on the tour. It may take fifteen or twenty minutes to get to the practice tee and by then I will have time only to hit about twenty or twenty-five shots, just enough to warm up. My caddy is already waiting for me there and I get into it quickly. First a few easy wedge shots, a few short and long irons, a couple of fairway woods, a couple of tee shots and then, ready or not, here I come. Now the cavalcade moves slowly toward the practice putting green where I like to spend a solid fifteen or twenty minutes. Here newspaper photographers or just plain golf fans ask me to pose for a picture. This is fun and I'm glad to do it, but, again, it takes time. When the clicking has stopped I fiddle around the putting green until I am called to the tee because stroking putts develops a soft, easy motion that gets a player into the right mood, the right frame of mind, to step on the tee and hit that first drive.

After the turmoil of the day, getting out on the course is like taking a nap. It is the first opportunity of the day to relax and be off by myself away from the crowds, the autograph books and the back slappers. I look for Betty, who is waiting just outside the putting green, give her a hug and step up to the starters' table and shake hands with the players I am paired with. If it is a good threesome we will have a big gallery. One of the first things we agree upon is that no one will give out autographs until the round is over. If one does it, the other two will have to do it too, or look like soreheads. Besides, we might never get back to the clubhouse. Each in turn steps up and hits his drive. We are off.

During the progress of a round not much is said. Some

players, like Bob Goalby or Marty Furgol, are pretty gabby. Others, like Snead, seldom say a word. Even when we talk it is usually no more than a comment on the other fellow's shot. Anything more than that might disturb someone's concentration, especially during a critical round. Now and then we talk about the weather, the golf course, or the good place we had dinner the night before. Occasionally, we even exchange jokes, but only if it won't distract from the job at hand. There is certainly none of the needling that will go on during a practice round. Some married players claim they can look right at their wives during a round and never see them. I'm sorry to say my concentration has never been that intense. I look for Betty frequently. Maybe just to make sure that she is out of the danger of one of my wild duck hooks off the tee. More often, just because I like to look at her.

Some days, when the round is over, a player will feel mentally bushed, but physically refreshed. This feeling usually follows a good round in which he has been thinking very well and scoring very well. Good thinking requires good concentration, both of which fatigue the brain. We are so delighted with our score, however, that physically we are capable of playing a game of basketball. In fact, I have done just that. One year while playing in the American Golf Classic at Akron I stayed with some friends in nearby Cuyahoga Falls. They had a basket in the backyard and after my round each day we would have a quick game of two-on-two before supper.

Then there are days when we come off the course feeling as if we had been out chopping wood for four nonstop hours. The mind is as fresh as a cold can of beer, mainly because it hasn't been used. But the body is thoroughly worn from having to blast the ball out of impossible situations which lazy thinking put it into.

When the round is over, it is not exceptional to find a hundred and fifty or two hundred people clamoring for autographs. They must sell the damn things. Then, if I have shot a good score and am leading the tournament, at least fifteen or twenty minutes will have to be spent in the press room. This is essential for accurate and informative newspaper coverage because the reporters will need facts that could be obtained only by coming out on the course once in a while. No one would ask them to go to that extreme. This kind of interview can be fun, but not for someone who has to do it all the time. It is a fresh experience for me, however, and I have a ball. For Arnold Palmer or Jack Nicklaus, say, it must be an interminable drag. The inquisition is the same city after city. Where were you born? How old are you? What do you weigh? When did you get married? Why did you get married? When did you win your first tournament? Do you think you can break up the Big Three (or the Big Two, or the Big Five, or the Big Ten)? I sit up on a platform and, if it is a big tournament, there will be twenty or thirty reporters down below firing questions up at me. There isn't much time to think, but who's thinking anymore?

When the press interview is over it is probably 6:30 or 7 o'clock and I am tired and hungry. Patient Betty is usually waiting for me outside. Her only consolation for this long wait is that she doesn't have to endure it often. I change back into my street shoes and then we head arm-in-arm for the parking lot. Even this takes a little time. There are still some fans around the clubhouse who shout a final good night and good luck. People just want to talk a bit, make a little contact somehow, and I like to accommodate them. Finally, after a short drive to the motel, I am back in the shower again. While I am drying off I make a few more phone calls, near duplicates of the ones I made in the morning, and by 8:30 or 9 o'clock Betty and I are ready for dinner. If I am just too exhausted to go out we order from room service and eat in the room. Otherwise we try to find a quiet, pleasant place nearby, have a cocktail before dinner and not talk too much about the golf tournament. After dinner it is back to the motel for some television watching and possibly a little reading before bedtime. I may read a mystery, or a popular novel. I hope I never find myself reading trash at night, meaning the so-called men's magazines. I think these are the biggest batch of garbage on the market and they have no place in an athlete's motel room or even in his mind. I know a few players on the tour who read this junk, but I can beat them all.

# 17 / The Open: fear at the summit

THE difference between the Masters and the U.S. Open is the difference between fun and fear. At Augusta you are playing aggressively to try to wrench a few birdies out of the golf course. The Open is played on a different course each year, but they all have severe similarities. The greens are slick and fast, the sand traps are as wide and as deep as bomb craters, the fairways are so narrow you could use them to conduct a sobriety test and the rough alongside each fairway and around each green is jungle-deep. In the Open you must play defensively for pars just to protect yourself from disaster on each hole. Telescoping all these problems is the fact that you must play the last 36 holes all on the same day. Let's face it. Most of us go into the Open just plain scared, but we are there because no sports event in the world can mean as much to its winner — in prestige, in money, in just plain ego-satisfaction — as the U.S. Open.

Doug Ford is certainly one of the toughest men on the tour and has been playing as a pro since 1950. During that time he has won nineteen tournaments, including the Masters and the PGA, and over $300,000 in prize money alone. Under pressure he is still regarded as one of the strongest players we've got, but in his reaction to the Open he proves to be no tougher than anybody else. He has never won it.

"Nothing can match the pressure to win that you find at the Open," he has admitted. "Every golfer there can feel the terrific tempo. You get all charged up like a kid about to enter his first tournament."

"Charged up" is another way of saying that you can feel Open Tension so strongly that it's with you from the very minute you come into town for the tournament until two or three days after it is over. You can feel the tension in a shortness of breath, a lack of appetite, restless nights and an overpowering desire to drink yourself to sleep in the evening. If you win, for the rest of your life you carry "U.S. Open champion" after your name and what this means forever to your ego and annually to your bank account can't be calculated accurately. Some have set a price on winning the title at $250,000, some put the figure higher. You can tell that the Open is coming up by the way the players start to joke about it. Their laughter rings with the false bravado of men about to go into battle. When they play their practice rounds they moan and groan about the course, they rave about how difficult it is. Everyone seems to expect a terrible round or two and tries to prepare himself for it. It is almost like a wake.

I have mentioned earlier what an Open title might have meant to a talented and popular personality like Mike Souchak. But history — golf history at any rate — is bulging with golfers with better records than Mike's who have never won the Open. You hear more about how Sam Snead *hasn't* won the Open than you do about the three Masters Championships he *has* won. Jimmy Demaret is one of the best golfers the United States has ever produced, but while winning three Masters himself he will never win the Open. Digging back a little farther in the record books you will find the names of Leo Diegel and MacDonald Smith, both golfers who won dozens and dozens of tournaments, came close many times in the Open, but never won. Snead is probably the greatest golfer never to win the Open, but Smith, Diegel and Demaret rank right behind him.

While anyone would certainly be proud to establish a record such as these golfers have made I certainly don't want to join them in their most unenviable category. Not too many players, however, often get the chance I had in 1963 to win this biggest of all titles. Between the Masters in April and the Open in June I had continued to play well. I planned to marry my fiancée, Betty Cline of Oklahoma City, in the fall. I had met Betty when she was working as a stewardess for American Airlines. It was 1961 and I was on a flight from Dallas to San Francisco. I gave her my usual line, we played a lot of gin rummy together and I let her win. I began to realize very soon, however, that she meant much more to me than any girl I had ever met. I saw quite a bit more of her during the next few months, we fell in love and decided to get married. We set a late 1963 date because it seemed a good idea to wait until the big part of the tournament season was over and to keep her working for a while. I was having serious troubles with my sponsor and I knew we could use the money.

When I picked up a check for $12,000 by finishing second in the Masters the picture changed. We decided to get married as soon as possible. I played at Greensboro just for old time's sake and then rushed on home, skipping the Houston and Texas Opens. We were married on April 28 in San Francisco and spent our honeymoon in Las Vegas while I played in the Tournament of Champions.

Every time a touring pro gets married he had better play well right away or he takes the razzing of his life. I knew I'd be in for it too, but I guess my play in the weeks following the wedding kept everyone quiet. As I mentioned earlier I tied Arnold for second at Las Vegas, finished fifth two shots back at the Colonial Invitation in Fort Worth. Skipped the Oklahoma City Open and then won the Memphis Open in a sudden death play-off with Tommy Aaron.

The Memphis Open was an important event for me. I had finished second several times, but it had been a long time since my last tournament victory and I was beginning to get a little depressed about playing so well, coming so close so often without being able to squeeze through the door. At this point I was third on the money winning list with a total of $36,000, surprising when you think I had not won a tournament. I was winning nothing but money and most of that was going to sponsor Crocker. At Memphis I started out with two 67's and led the tournament by two shots. Then it started to rain. It rained for two days and so the final two rounds were played on a Monday. When you are playing well and leading a tournament you want to get out on the golf course as fast as you can. Well, by the time we teed off on Monday I had been leading the tournament for four days. If ever a player figured to blow a lead it was me. It's tough to sit on one that long without being able to do something to protect it. And at Memphis all the top players, with the exception of Palmer, were on hand. I was paired with Tommy Aaron and Jerry Edwards the final two rounds and Tom was playing very well. By the time we had finished the sixteenth hole in the afternoon he had taken a two-shot lead on me.

The seventeenth hole at the Colonial Country Club in Memphis is a par three of 186 yards. Aaron, with the honor, hit a 4-iron that went dead for the flagstick all the way. The green is above the tee so you could not see the ball land, but I heard the crowd begin to cheer when it hit. Their applause died suddenly so I figured his shot had stopped well below the hole. I switched to a 3-iron and hit it just as well as I could. It flew deep into the green and the crowd's roar was explosive. I knew I was close. I was. Tom was 20 feet below the hole and my ball had stopped six feet to the left of it. Then he missed his putt and I made mine so we went to the last hole with me still a shot down. I thought I had a chance here because the eighteenth hole was a par five that I had a good chance to reach in two shots. My drive was long and I followed it with a 3-wood shot that landed in the center of the green about 20 feet to the left of the hole. Tommy wasn't too long off the tee, hit his second in the rough near a tree and came out beautifully, about 15 feet from the hole. My putt broke very sharply down the green, like a sickle blade, but I hit it well and I thought it was going to go right in for an eagle three. It rolled across the hole, however, and I settled for a birdie. When Tommy missed from 15 feet the tournament went into a sudden death play-off. I won the play-off when Tom hit his approach shot over the green and made a bogey five while I parred the hole. It was as if an immense weight had been lifted off my shoulders. I had not only produced two birdies in a row under great pressure, I had won the play-off too. Being something more than an also-ran supplied a strong enough dose of confidence to sustain me right through to the Open itself a month later.

Betty and I drove up to Boston after the Thunderbird Open outside New York. I hadn't played well there, but I was thinking about the U.S. Open, not the Thunderbird. Our drive was leisurely because it was the first time Betty had ever been in New England and I wanted her to have a good look. What she got was a good look at the New England Thruway. We arrived at our hotel, the Ritz-Carlton, too late for me to play a practice round on Monday, but I went out Tuesday afternoon for my first look at the course. When I came back to the hotel late that afternoon I was in a state of shock. I couldn't believe that a course could be so hard. I don't know what I scored, but it must have been in the middle 80's. The next day I began to play a little better, stayed close to par, and so I felt in reasonably good shape for the tournament.

For those who played on it during the 1963 Open, The Country Club in Brookline, Massachusetts, will always be memorable. We will probably have nightmares about it for the rest of our lives. It possessed the usual Open characteristics such as fast greens, deep rough and narrow fairways, but the course had three other things that also contributed to the highest winning score since 1935. First of all The Country Club is a very old-fashioned course. This means a lot of mounds, a lot of hills, plenty of bunkers and smallish, circular greens. It also means a great many holes on which you cannot see the flagstick from the fairway. Occasionally a glimpse of the flag itself was visible, flapping like a yellow handkerchief in the strong breeze, but there were at least 12 holes that could be called blind or partially blind. This meant that when you teed off, or when you hit your approach shot, you could not be *exactly* sure where you should be hitting the ball. On the first hole the green sat in a little hollow behind a raised road and only the tippy-top of the stick and the bright bit of yellow at the top of the pin could be seen. From the tee of the second hole, a long par three, just the upper portion of the flagstick was visible. The third hole, a long par four with water behind the green and traps all around it, featured a huge mound on the right side of the fairway. It was very difficult to drive the ball anywhere except directly behind this mound and so you were firing your second shot at blue sky, not at an actual target. On the fourth and fifth holes, both par fours, the flagstick was out of sight of the tee and a player had only a hazy idea of where to place the tee shot for the best approach shot into the hole. The sixth hole was short, but the green sat so high above where the tee shots were landing that a long climb up the hill was required in order to get a specific idea about what target you should aim at. The second shot was a delicate wedge shot of about 50 yards, and with nothing but the top of the flagstick to hit at all perception of depth was destroyed. You just pitched and prayed. On the seventh, a long par three, the green rolled away from the tee and the bottom of the flagstick was obscured. This made it difficult to be precise about what club to use. On the eighth hole the green, again, sat high above where the drives were landing. No one could be sure that he was hitting his approach shot anywhere near the hole. The ninth hole presented the same problem. Unless you could get up very close to the green on this par five in two shots, just about impossible for anybody in the field, you were hitting a delicate little pitch shot with only a vague sense of accuracy. On the tenth was another blind green. The only target most of us could see from the fairway was a tree well behind the green that could be lined up directly above and behind the flagstick. That's what you were aiming at and it made it extremely difficult to tell just how hard or how softly to hit the approach shot. The eleventh green, guarded by a pond and at the end of a fairway tightly flanked by trees, was invisible from the tee. The entire green on the 470-yard par four twelfth hole was invisible from the fairway. We were just swinging away like blind men. The thirteenth, fourteenth, fifteenth, sixteenth and seventeenth holes were more or less straight away, but the finishing hole, 18, was partially blind. The green was elevated about six or eight feet and usually buried in the shade of the elm trees that surrounded it. It was very difficult to make out the exact location of the flagstick. We could only see the top half of it and even that was partially obscured by shadows.

These probably sound like the gripes of a sore loser — maybe they are — but I am also trying to point out one reason why the scores were so high. The course, as they say, was the same for everyone. The player who adjusted best to the conditions was the one who had the best chance of winning. There were also two other reasons why the Open of 1963 was a harder test than the pros had faced in many years; undoubtedly harder than any we will have to take again for many years. After a particularly bitter winter and a particularly dry spring, the course was not in good shape. The grass on a great many of the greens had been recently resown. This created very inconsistent putting surfaces. Usually a competitor can count on the fact that Open greens will be fast greens. At Brookline they were all fast, but some were so much faster than others that a great deal of guesswork was involved. The fairways, too, were not in good condition. A disease called winterkill, caused by the sun burning through a winter's accumulation of ice, had made the grass on the fairways extremely ragged. You could not depend on a good lie. The result was heavy lies in the fairways and shots that were difficult to control.

Who will forget the wind? What a howling ordeal that was on the final day. You almost had to envy those, including the defending champion Jack Nicklaus, who had missed the 36-hole cut and had gone home. Not only was the wind strong, but it blew first in one direction and then another. On the last afternoon I was standing on the tee of the par three sixteenth hole waiting to hit and trying to figure out what club to use. I plucked some grass from the tee and flipped it into the air to check the wind direction. The grass rose slowly and straight upward. We were on the television camera at the time. The gallery that surrounded the tee, and everyone watching TV got a laugh. They could appreciate at home the problem we were facing on the course.

Given the nightmare conditions that prevailed it is hardly surprising that Julius Boros trudged placidly through the three days of horror and came out the winner. Under the very toughest of conditions Jay is at his best. I have been paired with him on several occasions, in important tournaments and in the Ryder Cup matches. He is a fine putter and the fact that he hits the ball on a very low trajectory stands him in good stead when the wind is blowing hard as it was at Brookline. Jay wouldn't get flustered if you punched him in the belly as he reached the top of his backswing. While Arnold Palmer seems to love pressure and thrive on it, while the rest of us are usually rattled by it, pressure is something that Boros just ignores.

The character of the U.S. Open had changed considerably between the time I first played in it at Rochester in 1956 and my third championship in 1963. First of all, the overall purse had jumped in seven years from $24,000 (a figure of vast insignificance on the tour today where a tournament winner can often pocket as much as that) to $86,000. I haven't checked the ratings with the TV networks that have telecast the Open over the years, but I know that seven years ago the Open was something you watched only because you were curious to see how golf looked on television. Now you watch it because you are determined to see for yourself how the U.S. Open is going to come out.

Strangely enough the cast of characters hasn't changed that much — though there are certainly some significant additions.

[ 225 ]

A great many of the players I goggled at like a stagestruck kid in 1956 are still very much around. Cary Middlecoff, who won that year, is much less active. But the man who tied Ben Hogan, now retired, for second was none other than the 1952 and 1963 winner, Julius Boros. Ted Kroll tied for fourth at Rochester, Arnold Palmer finished seventh and Venturi finished eighth after an opening-round 77. He was the low-amateur. Doug Ford, Jerry Barber, Billy Maxwell, Bill Casper, and Jay Hebert all finished in the top twenty in 1956. Snead, Bolt and Souchak all played the final day and so did Walter Burkemo, Gene Littler, Frank Stranahan, Bob Rosburg, and Bo Wininger. Tony Lema was the pro finishing with the highest score, a 308, but I did manage to finish a stroke ahead of amateur John Garrett. Where the Open, or any major championship is involved, the only significant additions to that cast since 1956 have been Jack Nicklaus and Gary Player.

The greatest change over that period of time has been a change in the climate of the game. Winning the Open in 1956 meant more than a little prestige, but really nothing compared to what it means today. Don't confuse the statement with fresh news when I say that golf is currently played for very high stakes — not just what they give away on the site of the tournament, but also what the magnetic force of a major title will draw in. It is also a fact, however, that golf is not a game designed to be played under this kind of pressure. It is a game for a pleasant day, with only a quiet group of friends to play with you and no pressure but the satisfaction of turning in a good score. It is a game of extreme delicacy, where there is little margin for error. Every mistake can punish you, can add to your score. When a man is trying to play this delicate game in the hothouse pressure of cheering crowds, gaping TV cameras and hundreds of thousands of dollars at stake, the man and his golf game can crack as easily as a crystal finger bowl. It takes a very special kind of man to win the big tournaments today. A relentless, aggressive Arnold Palmer, for instance. A phlegmatic Julius Boros or Jack Nicklaus. Or someone with the calm assurance of Billy Casper. It is astonishing when someone as high-strung as Gary Player is able to win a major championship and yet Player has won two of them, the Masters and the PGA. It is a testimony not only to his fine ability as a golfer, but also to his strong will. I'm not sure I'm really cut out for this game either. I should be playing something like football or basketball, where I have a chance to run and shout and very little time to think about the consequences of what I have done or will do. There is too much time on those long walks between shots to think about yourself, the other players, the danger that lies ahead, the disastrous results of stumbling into that danger; of the hero you will be if you successfully negotiate the danger, the choke-up artist you will be called if you do not; of your wife who is walking along with you, but somewhere hidden in the gallery; of your friends who are watching on television; of the score you must shoot to win and of the putt that you just missed on the last hole. Above all you are thinking about the drama of being on stage, of being a vital figure in a big-time production like a U.S. Open or a Masters tournament. These are not the thoughts you should be wrestling with when you are trying to hit a little white ball into a little black hole.

All of these things effect most of us in the major championships. They were especially present in my mind and my guts as the 1963 U.S. Open drew into its climatic stages. The final day was very sunny and very windy. I had played well and the night before had left Betty back in the hotel with a book and had gone out with Fred Corcoran to watch the Boston Red Sox massacre the New York Yankees in a night game at Fenway Park. I left before the game was over and was in bed, asleep, by midnight. I had reason to sleep well. I was not leading the tournament, I was three shots back of Jacky Cupit, Palmer, and Finsterwald in fact, but I was playing extremely well, driving especially well, and felt confident of my ability to win. I didn't care who else was going to be out there against me. In the morning I shot a 74, not a bad round considering the wind, and it moved me up within a shot of the leader, Jacky Cupit. It would have been a much better round if I hadn't gone to lunch four holes sooner than I should have, bogeying three easy holes — the 420-yard fifteenth, the 175-yard sixteenth, and the 365-yard seventeenth — right in a row. These are potential birdie holes and I was a little upset that I had done so badly on them, but over a morning's play I had actually gained ground on the leaders. At one point, in fact, before I missed a putt of eight feet on the fifteenth green, I was actually tied with Cupit for the lead. I had a quick lunch with Betty in the grill of the clubhouse, three glasses of milk and some meatloaf, went over to the locker room to change my shoes and before I knew it was out on the course again. As I played through the front nine I felt a serenity that is seldom with me. Everything seemed to be falling into place. I seemed to be fated to win. I made one bogey and eight pars and so went to the tenth tee still one shot back of Cupit, who was playing about two holes behind me; two shots ahead of Palmer, who was directly behind me; and a shot ahead of Boros, who was directly in front of me. On 10 I hit a drive well down the center of the fairway, but my 6-iron approach shot skipped over the green and left me not too far from the hole, but in very deep grass. I chipped poorly, missed a 10-foot putt for a bogey five. Even this did not bother me unduly because I felt I would play 11 and 12 in par and the others would have trouble with at least one of these holes — just as I had. Right in front of me on the eleventh, Boros hit into the water short of the green and took a double-bogey six. I figured he was out of the tournament.

I did manage pars on the next two holes and then gave close scrutiny to the big scoreboard by the thirteenth tee. I was eight over par for the tournament, Palmer was nine over and Cupit, who had not yet bogeyed the eleventh and twelfth holes, was still only six over par. The thirteenth, downhill but into the wind, played long. I reached the green 20 feet from the hole with a drive and a 4-iron. Walter Burkemo, my playing partner, was a little closer than that so I putted first and rolled the ball about 18 inches past the hole.

"Do you mind waiting while I putt out?" I asked Walter, then stood over my putt and missed it. It went all the way around the hole and stayed out. Woof! That was like being punched in the groin by Sonny Liston. You say to yourself, "No, no, it didn't happen. Let me putt it again and make it all right." But of course this isn't possible. There is nothing in golf as irrevocable as a missed putt. From my point of view this changed the entire complexion of the tournament. Now I was three shots back (I did not know that Cupit had bogeyed 11 by this time or that he would bogey 12) and I thought I absolutely must play a forcing game to see if I couldn't win back some of these strokes. I could not wait for Cupit to give them back. My attempt was almost successful, but I had begun to lose a little confidence in my putting after the thirteenth. I was just short of the par five fourteenth hole in two shots, chipped up about eight feet away and then missed my putt for a birdie. I parred the fifteenth and then took another look at the scoreboard by the fifteenth green. I was nine over par, Boros was 11 over par, Cupit was now eight over par and Palmer, right behind me on the course, was tied with me at nine over par for the tournament. It had happened. No one was catching up with Cupit but he was coming back to us. The scores were bunching up, but with some easy holes to go the time had come to go after Cupit. I knew I had to do something on one of the three closing holes.

The finishing holes at Brookline were played through a shouting, groaning corridor of people, four deep. They were lined up on all sides, from the fifteenth fairway procession be-eenth green. It made for a raucous, twisting procession because the holes doubled back on each other. The fifteenth hole points due east, the sixteenth goes off at right angles to the left, the seventeenth comes straight back toward the fifteenth green, then turns sharply toward the east again. The eighteenth hole comes straight back toward the clubhouse just south of the fifteenth green and fairway. The scene was like something from a Cecil B. DeMille movie of ancient Rome. We were the Roman legions marching through the crowded boulevards and the crowds were cheering themselves hoarse. The only props missing were the bands and the elephants.

When Boros birdied the sixteenth hole just ahead of me I was not too alarmed because he was still a shot behind me. I checked the wind, and that was when it blew the grass straight up into the air. Then I hit a 5-iron shot to within 12 feet of the hole. Again I hit a poor putt. It would have gone straight in if I'd hit it hard enough, but I tapped it too lightly and it slid off to the right of the hole. I went over to the next tee and hit as perfect a tee shot as I could. It was well down the center of the fairway and left me with about a 7-iron to the green.

By the time I was ready to hit that shot, however, the entire tournament picture had altered radically. As I walked toward my tee shot, some 240 yards from the tee, I heard a violent eruption of sound from the sixteenth green behind me. Palmer obviously, had birdied the hole and was now a shot ahead of me. I had hardly walked another 25 yards before there was another roar from the gallery around the fifteenth green. Cupit had chipped in from the edge of the green for a birdie that put him two shots ahead of me and one ahead of Palmer. Up ahead of me on the green was Boros and, as I watched and waited for my turn to hit, he knocked in a 20-foot putt to put him square with me.

Well, I was hardly feeling serene and confident by this time. I was feeling slightly desperate. I just knew I had to birdie the last two holes now to stand any kind of chance. This desperation, I think, came from inexperience. I have played in very few major championships. Last year's Open, in fact, was only the second major tournament in which I had ever been in contention. At my first Open in 1956 I was just a green kid who didn't even know what was happening. I didn't play in another Open until 1962 and then I had been driving so badly that I played my tee shots with a 3-wood and missed the cut. I had played in my first PGA in 1962, but had had to drop out at the beginning of the third round with a sore hand. In the spring of '63 I had played in only my first Masters. Now here I was standing in the seventeenth fairway with everyone making birdies around me and the crowds yelling as if they were at a bullfight. I had counted myself out of the tournament and thought that nothing short of a miracle could ever bring me home in front. As it turned out if I had parred the last two holes I would have been in the play-off too. With a little more experience I might have realized that the other contenders might be about to take a little of the gas, too, under the tremendous pressure of trying to win such a tournament. Looking at the seventeenth I figured I had a 7-iron shot to the green, but I wanted to get the ball as close to the hole as possible. I used a 6-iron instead and tried to cut it in toward the hole with a left-to-right fade. I hit it off somewhat of a sloping lie, however, and instead of fading it went dead straight, took a big hop off the green and high up the side of a sand trap directly behind the green. I had to stand up in the trap and I was slipping down toward the ball, creating the danger of moving it and incurring a two-stroke penalty. I knew that it was curtains in the Open for me. I hit it as quickly as I could, blasted it over the green and had to chip the ball back stiff for a bogey five. I drove into the rough on the last hole and bogeyed it too. I signed my card, put my head down and trudged into the locker room. On television I watched Palmer miss a short putt to bogey the seventeenth hole, watched Cupit hit a series of bad shots and bad putts to double-bogey the seventeenth hole and blow the tournament, and watched as both Cupit and Palmer made nice pars on the last hole to tie Boros for first, all with a nine-over-par 293.

How easy it might have been for me to tie Boros too was not the kind of thing I wanted to think about. I changed my shoes, threw my gear into my bag and rushed out to meet Betty by our car. As I came out of the locker room a drunk dressed in worn Boston tweeds and a striped tie tottered over.

"Hey, Champagne Tony," he shouted. "What happened to Champagne Tony?"

Then he clapped me on the back hard enough to break it and ambled off chuckling to himself. I was apoplectic with rage, dropped my bag flat on the driveway pavement and felt that I was just about to rip his head off. God only knows where I got the strength to hold off.

The U.S. Open about ended the competitive year as far as I was concerned. I tied for first at the $110,000 Cleveland Open the following week, but I was floating along on sheer inertia. I tied for thirteenth at the PGA Championship at hothouse Dallas in July, but my showing was a triumph of good fortune over bad playing. I stumbled through a miscellaneous assortment of other tournaments and did not get my competitive juices going again until the Ryder Cup matches against Great Britain in October. My life was changing. So much was taking place off the golf course that it became difficult to remain excited about hitting the little white ball. And yet, hitting the little white ball was what started it all in the first place and — if I was lucky — would keep it going.

# 18 / TV, Arnold Palmer and other splendors

THE summer of 1963 would have dwindled to an anticlimax for me except that I got an additional taste of international golfing competition: in September against Formosa's Chen Ching-Po on Shell's *Wonderful World of Golf* television show, filmed in Japan; in October during the biennial Ryder Cup matches against the British, held in Atlanta, Georgia.

Appearing on a filmed TV golf match is like being asked to act your way through the Battle of the Bulge. Everything is legitimate, aboveboard and strictly realistic, but the golfer must walk through his real-life role in a very specific way. Shortly after the Masters tournament in April the Shell people had asked me to appear on their show and I requested that I be scheduled to play in Japan. I wanted Betty to get a look at the Far East and I wanted to see how it had changed in the eight years since my last visit. The Shell show is filmed in color and always matches a good U.S. pro against an outstanding professional of another country. The match is usually played in the latter's general geographic area.

Chen and I played at the Fuji course just outside of Eto. The club is located atop high cliffs overlooking the Pacific Ocean and the course is dotted with beautiful pine trees and colorful foliage of all sorts. It is immaculately groomed, but the grass on the fairways and the greens is needle sharp. It was like playing golf across the bristles of a hairbrush. Japan was between typhoons at that time of year so we had to get the 18-hole match over with in a hurry. It only took us two days; four holes the first day, fourteen the next.

Shell, in contrast to the other shows, does a very thorough production job. Nothing except the golf itself is left to chance. Even part of the gallery is hired so that it can be maneuvered around the course, told where to stand and when to applaud. It takes about forty-five minutes to play each hole because six cameras are used to film the match and they must be relocated after each shot. When a player hits his drive he does not simply walk after his ball as he would in a normal round of golf; he must wait until the gallery has received its instructions and the cameras have been moved down the fairway. Only when everything and everyone is in his proper place, and the assistant director has called, "Ready," would Chen and I come striding off the tee and on down the fairway. Once we reached our shots we faced another fifteen- or twenty-minute wait while the cameras were moved into position to catch from various angles the picture of the approach shot coming into the green. At these intervals a girl caddy, assigned to this special duty, would whip out a folding camp chair so that Chen and I could sit down and relax. Eventually the director would call, "Okay, we are just about ready." Up we'd get, the girl would fold up the chairs, whisk them away and leave us standing at the ready by our caddies. When the director would wave his hand we would go through a pantomime of consultation about what club to use (although we had known exactly which club for at least ten minutes), draw it out of the bag and then hit the shot as the cameras whirred. The noise of the cameras is a little bothersome at first, but since they start grinding a long time before you start swinging, eventually you become accustomed to them.

The only thing that you never get accustomed to is taking twelve hours to play a round of golf.

Chen and I played an exciting match. He birdied the first two holes to jump off to a two-shot lead, but I had drawn even by the sixth and took a one-shot lead on the fourteenth. The outcome eventually revolved around the seventeenth hole, one of the toughest golf holes I have ever seen. It is 450 yards long and slopes upward toward a green guarded in front by two cavernous traps, one directly behind the other. In the middle of the fairway is a camelback mound that tends to kick the tee shot down onto either side of the fairway. I still held my one-stroke lead and both Chen and I drove about a foot off the edge of the fairway into the rough. But his ball rolled into a good lie while I drew one down under some weeds. We waited several minutes while the cameras were moved and then Chen hit his second shot just above the top edge of the first trap. To make his par four he was left with a simple, short chip straight into the middle of the green. When my turn came to hit I flew my approach squarely into the middle of the first trap. For fifteen minutes thereafter, while the cameras were shifted again and one of them moved in for a close-up of my lie in the sand, I smoked a number of cigarettes, but was damned if I was going to sit in my camp chair. I was faced with an explosion of about thirty yards that must clear the second deep bunker. Fifteen minutes is a long time to contemplate a shot like that. As it turned out, I hit well over the second bunker to within 12 feet of the hole. Now it was Chen's turn to wait and fidget. After what must have been an endless ten minutes, he got the okay to hit. Then he fluffed his simple chip, left it 20 feet short of the hole and we both made bogey fives. I held my lead with a good par on the last hole and beat him 69 to 70.

As Betty and I flew back from the Orient I was looking forward to the Ryder Cup matches with an eagerness I hadn't felt in years. Making the team, of course, gives a golfer a tremendous sense of accomplishment. He has been named to it through his performance on the tour over a two-year period. It is an achievement that gives him an important place in the history of golf, however far he may eventually fade from the week-to-week tournament scene. More vitally it gives the ten players selected a chance to rise above the self centered existence of life on the tour and, if only in a small way, serve as representatives of their country. There is no money involved in playing in the Ryder Cup matches but, though we are all professionals, it is a duty we feel deeply honored to perform.

Ryder Cup invitations are based on a strict point system, extending over a two-year period. Only five-year members of the PGA are eligible to play (Jack Nicklaus, therefore, was ineligible in 1963). At each official PGA tournament the winner receives 70 points toward a Ryder Cup berth (provided he is a five-year man), second place 42 points, third 28 points, fourth 21 points, fifth 18 points, sixth 14 points, seventh 11 points, and eighth, ninth and tenth, 10, 8 and 6 points, respectively. The PGA champion (provided he is eligible) is an automatic qualifier and the point system is also scaled upward in this tournament.

The 1963 team included myself, Arnold Palmer, Bill Casper, Julius Boros, Billy Maxwell, Johnny Pott, Bob Goalby, Dow Finsterwald, Dave Ragan and Gene Littler. At our first meeting following the 1963 PGA Championship in Dallas we had unanimously elected Arnold Palmer as our captain. This meant that he would decide which eight of the ten-man team would play each day and who would be paired with whom. This and other duties make it a considerable responsibility.

But Palmer's leadership represented another reason why I looked forward to the matches so expectantly. For the first time in my life I would have a chance to play *for* Arnold Palmer instead of against him.

Arnold is certainly my choice as the best golfer in the world. I have never gone in for idolizing any single person, but if I do have an idol it is Palmer. It seems odd even to me to idolize a man that I butt heads with in earnest every week, but it is simply a fact of life. I am not alone in this sentiment. Palmer is highly respected by every player on the tour because, in addition to being such a magnificent golfer, he is a very down-to-earth person. He was thoughtful and unselfish when he first came out on the tour and his spectacular success has not changed him at all. Most of the touring pros agree that if fate has decreed one man must dominate our profession, then we are happy this role is played by Arnold. No one could represent us more ably.

The first contact I had with Palmer took place just prior to the Buick Open in 1958 when I had been out on the course in violation of tournament procedure practicing sand shots by the third green. His genuine thoughtfulness in pointing out my lack of it seemed so remarkable to me that I became one of his most ardent admirers on the spot.

Palmer's consideration for others goes beyond just talk. Prior to the 1960 Masters tournament, which Palmer eventually won with that miraculous birdie-birdie finish that beat Venturi by a stroke, a group of us had gone up to Crystal River, Florida, for a short vacation. This is a resort development on the Gulf north of St. Petersburg that contains facilities for boating, fishing and golf. There were about a half dozen of us there including Palmer. Most of the players were planning to stay for a while and then head directly to Augusta

for the Masters. I had not rated a trip to the Masters and
so I planned to go to Wilmington, North Carolina, and compete in the Azalea Open, which is usually the last stop before
Augusta. I had no way of getting from Crystal River to the
nearby airport so Arnold agreed to drive me over. Well, we
were all out in a boat on one of the salt water inlets — skin
diving, fishing and sea horsing around in general — when suddenly I had missed my plane. I rushed back to shore, got on
the telephone and eventually booked a reservation on a flight
out of St. Petersburg. This meant a drive of ninety miles from
Crystal River. Word went out to the boat and Arnold came
right in, we packed up his car and took off on a trip that
would take him four hours to complete. It never occurred to
him not to make it. He not only took me straight to the airport, but also waited there until he saw me get on the plane
and off the ground. His main concern was that I make the
flight. If I had not, I'm sure he would have turned right
around and driven me up to Atlanta. Anything to get me on
a plane headed for Wilmington and my next tournament.

Arnold's thoughtfulness spills over even when he is competing vigorously on the golf course and his attitude brings
out the best golf in everyone he is paired with. He possesses
a special quality that is missing in the rest of us. Long before the last round of the 1963 Tournament of Champions at
Las Vegas the outcome had been determined — at least as far
as the winner was concerned. Bill Casper had been trailing
leader Jack Nicklaus by a couple of shots after 62 holes, but
had been forced to quit because of a bad hand. With Bill
out of the tournament Jack suddenly had a fat six-shot lead
over the rest of us. Palmer had been paired with Casper, but
he played on alone and when he caught up with Bob Goalby
and myself after the eleventh hole he simply joined us and

made it a threesome. At that point I was two shots back of Palmer in the struggle for second place, but I birdied the twelfth, the fifteenth and seventeenth while he birdied 15, to tie him as we went to the last tee. The difference between second and third place meant $2500 in prize money so that is what the outcome of the hole was worth to each of us. The eighteenth at the Desert Inn Country Club is a 445-yard par four, featuring a large pond along the right side. My tee shot carried a little past Arnold's so he had to hit his approach shot first. He hit it a trifle strong and it rolled to the back edge of the green about 50 feet from the hole. Then, hitting mine not quite as firmly, I stuck the ball about 15 feet just below the hole. I had a very makable birdie putt and Arnie had to hit his down the green and over a rise some 12 feet his side of the hole. His putt was a great one. It came skidding down the green, over the rise and just sort of oozed across the left edge of the cup. I stood there with my mouth open and my eyes hanging out. Then I looked up and Arnold was coming across the green, hitching up his pants the way he does when things are going his way, and looking at me. He had a grin as big as a slice of watermelon on his face and it said as clearly as words could have, "Aha, you s.o.b., I almost got you there, didn't I." Then he started to laugh at the look of shock still on my face and I laughed too. I just barely missed the putt that would have beaten him for second place. It was worth some brief needling later. We are friends, but there we were on the golf course knifing each other just as hard as we could for that second-place finish.

I was also paired with Arnold during the fourth round of the $110,000 1963 Cleveland Open which Palmer eventually won. I had bogeyed two holes near the end of the third round and had fallen back into a tie with Nicklaus and Palmer.

I felt a little apprehensive about having to beat out both of them. Late on the final day Jack had dropped out of contention, but Tommy Aaron, playing well ahead of us, had birdied the last four holes and was in the clubhouse with a 273. Arnold and I both missed birdie putts on the fourteenth hole and as we looked at the scoreboard on our way to the fifteenth tee realized that each of us would need a birdie on one of the last four holes to beat Aaron. We were shooting for a $22,000 first prize, but at that point Arnold turned to me and said an odd thing — odd for a professional golfer, that is, but very nice and typical of Arnie. "It would almost be fun to tie with you, Tony," he said. "We could have such a good match tomorrow. But now let's play just as hard as we can." We did, but neither of us was able to get the necessary birdie.

As it turned out Aaron, Palmer and I had to play off the next day. Arnie was red-hot and for a while it looked as if he were going to break the course record. Tommy and I, however, weren't getting down any birdie putts and Arnie was way out in front. And then a strange thing happened. Tom and I began to make birdies when we came on TV at the fifteenth hole and Arnold began to make bogies. It was very unlike Arnold. When the TV cameras are on he is one of golf's great showmen. That's when he begins to play super golf. As anyone knows who may have been watching, he was showman enough to give both Tommy and me a sound licking. We simply never caught him.

This friendly, but fiercely competitive attitude of Arnold's was clearly visible at the Ryder Cup matches, held in October at the East Lake Country Club in Atlanta. Thirty-two matches are played during a three-day period. Each match is worth one point to the winning country and a tied match yields half a point to each side. The atmosphere reeks with international and diplomatic goodwill. Winning is supposedly the least important reason for being there, although each country, obviously, wants very much to do so. Arnold Palmer of the U.S.A. especially.

"Fellows," he said, when he spoke to us at our first get-together in Atlanta, "wouldn't it be just great if we could win this thing 32 to 0?"

There never was much chance for a shutout. The British team was too talented and too stubborn and the Americans were so tense I was afraid our nerves wouldn't last out the week. I was getting pretty jumpy a few days before the event started, but on the final morning the tension hit me like a bucket of cold water. At 7:50 A.M. members of both teams assembled on the putting green. A large crowd was on hand and so was a marching band. First the United States flag was pulled up the flagpole and the band played the "Star-Spangled Banner." Then the British flag, to the tune of "God Save the Queen," was hoisted. When I heard the music and saw the flags of our two nations, for the first time I felt the full impact of why we were here. Our job was not only to maintain the close and friendly contact that we enjoy with Great Britain, but also to conduct ourselves in a sportsmanlike fashion, and to put on a display of first class, championship golf, and last but not least, to maintain our sense of humor. It was a tall order. During the course of the week I could tell that everyone was as nervous as I was. We talked to each other, but the words didn't make sense and no one really listened to them anyway. Our backswings were too fast and when we putted our heads swayed like metronomes.

The Ryder Cup competition is interesting for more reasons than the fact that it is a big international event. First of all, it is contested at match play, meaning on a hole by hole basis, something that the U.S. pros engage in only during practice rounds. Secondly, the method of play for the first day's matches is in a form we seldom encounter: the Scotch foursome. Each nation is represented by four two-man teams, but each team plays only one ball. One player will drive off the odd-numbered tees and his partner off the even-numbered ones. They proceed to hit alternate shots thereafter. The luck of the play, therefore, will often dictate that one player does not hit an iron shot or a putt for possibly two holes in succession. Then suddenly he is faced with a critical and tricky five-foot putt that he has just about forgotten how to hit.

It also puts a weird sort of pressure on each man. I was partnered with Julius Boros for both of our 18-hole rounds the first day, and it seemed that every time he drove the ball into the fairway I would whack the next shot into the woods. On the seventh hole Bob Jones, who is a member of the East Lake Club, drove out in a golf cart to watch us play. This really put me into an emotional bind. We were playing a tight match with Neil Coles, whose long curly hair makes him look like one of the Three Stooges, and tall, blond, tousle-haired Bernard Hunt. Boros was driving on the odd-numbered holes and had put his tee shot smack in the middle of the fairway. I had a 5-iron in my hand when I spotted Jones watching us and I thought, "I'm going to show him a golf shot." I intended to fade the ball softly into the green, but in my excitement I not only pulled the shot off to the left, but I hooked it as well. It ended up so deep among the trees that poor Julie couldn't even get it to the green.

The final score of the 1963 Ryder Cup matches was 23–9 in our favor, but the event was much more closely contested than that. The British won only six of the thirty-two matches outright, but ten of the remaining matches went to the final hole and sixteen of them at least to the seventeenth green. I was also considerably impressed by the British golfing temperament. I had always been led to believe that the British were a dry, stiff-upper-lip sort of nation. That preconceived notion was thoroughly shattered during my very enjoyable match with Peter Alliss on the afternoon of the final day.

Alliss, a tall, dark-haired Londoner, had defeated Palmer in the morning, one up, and seemed to be on his stick. At the second hole of a match that we eventually halved, I hit a good shot onto the green fairly close to the cup. Alliss had also hit his second shot onto the green, but a good 35 or 40 feet from the hole. Then he stroked his putt into the hole for a birdie three. As he walked across the green to retrieve his ball he rolled his eyes, looked over at me and announced clearly, "I *am* sorry."

The crowd that was jammed around the green laughed uproariously and so did I. As far as I was concerned this was the high point of the 1963 Ryder Cup matches.

It is also one of the many high points during my life as a touring professional. Peter Alliss, rolling his eyes and saying he is sorry; Arnold Palmer almost sinking a long putt and then hitching up his trousers and grinning at me as he strides across the green; Jim Ferree wearing a silly little straw hat and captivating galleries in Vancouver while winning his only big tournament; Tommy Jacobs under the engine of our car the night before his first big victory; Don Whitt dancing on the hotel patio during fiesta in Panama; Gerry Priddy smashing 7-irons across a Florida waterway; Jack Nicklaus barely holing the putt that beat me in the Masters; Chick Harbert lecturing me on the fourteenth tee at St. Petersburg; Dow Finsterwald lecturing me in the hotel room at St. Paul; Venturi weeping when Palmer won the Masters; Caddy Wally Heron and I exchanging happy smiles when I have hit a good shot; the explosive roar of the gallery watching a long putt drop; or my wife Betty sleeping as I get out of bed at dawn. These are all parts of life on the pro tour. They don't sound like much, but they add up. The opportunity to earn big money is not the only factor that brings young men and old out onto the professional tour. Most of us just love the game, and the tour represents a way to play it every day and still make a living.

Playing the tour presents two very compelling challenges that so many of us find impossible to resist, challenges that have nothing to do with money. First of all, for pro and amateur alike, there is the challenge of the game itself. Golf requires a technique that none of us ever quite master, but which we all think we could master with just a little more playing and a little more practice. In our effort to reach this unreachable perfection we become very much like hounds at the dog track. We are chasing a rabbit that we are never going to catch, but this is what makes the game so fascinating, so hypnotic. We all know that we are never going to catch the rabbit, but we are getting a terrific bang out of trying. Everything takes second place to the chase. A job that keeps you at a desk from 9 o'clock in the morning to 5 o'clock at night — Lord, what a bind! Happiness is a fine day and a fine golf course. A non-golfing girl I know once said that she thought the greatest torture God could devise for a golfer would be to one day empower him to hit every drive, every iron and every putt perfectly. Imagine his anguish when, returned to his mortal golfing self, he tries to play again. Well, every golfer has actually had these moments. The hacker who suddenly fired a burst of seven straight pars that seemed as effortless as breathing. The really good amateur who breaks the course record one day and decides he could really play this game well if he could play it more often. The desire to play and play and play and play becomes overwhelming. For some there is no solution to this problem. For others there is the pro tour.

The second powerful lure of the tour is the clean and un-complicated nature of the competitive challenge it presents. I guess a few no-talent actresses have gotten good parts be-cause the producer had the hots for them. I guess a few good baseball players never got a real chance to show their wares because the manager could not stand them. I guess a few quarterbacks were made to look bad because their teammates wouldn't block for them. I guess a few junior executives be-came senior executives because they could play office politics. Well, you can't win golf tournaments by playing politics. Once you have put your ball down on the first tee no one can hold you back but yourself. No one is allowed to help you but your caddy. Some of us complain about our luck or our putting, but we know that luck and putting are part of the game that we have chosen to play for a living. We also know, and be-lieve me it is a very satisfying and rewarding piece of knowl-edge, that we will get out of the game what we put into it. That we will progress in our chosen profession just as far as our physical equipment and our dedication will take us. When a tournament professional shoots a good round of golf that round belongs to him and him alone. When he shoots a bad round of golf he surely wishes that it did not belong to him, but he knows within himself that there is no one else to blame; not a selfish producer, an irascible manager, a jealous vice president, or a line that won't block for him. In tournament golf everything is right out there in the open. In the long run the best player — and when I say the best I mean in every department: skill, nerve, and temperament — is going to shoot the best scores, win the most tournaments, make the most money. That is the way life should be, really, and yet so seldom is. But that is the way of life on the pro tour.

*Afterword*
*by*
*Dave Anderson*

*I never knew Tony Lema, but it seems as if I did. The night after the 1972 British Open at Muirfield ended, I was having dinner with Fred Corcoran in Edinburgh at a small sidestreet restaurant. Even before I ordered salmon, he was talking about the golfer who had died at age 32 in a 1966 plane crash, two years after "Golfers' Gold" had been published, two years after Champagne Tony had won the British Open.*

*"He would've been one of the great ones," Fred said.*

*Fred Corcoran was not completely impartial. He had been Tony's business manager, but Tony had been more than a client. Tony was a friend of the family. In a fly-swatting contest one day with little Judy Corcoran, then 12 years old, the golfer won.*

*"You swatted 20 more flies than I did," Judy said. "I owe you 20 cents."*

*"No, only 16 cents," Tony said. "Your father always takes 20 percent."*

*Fred Corcoran, of course, had been much more than a business manager. He knew golf and he knew golfers. He had helped form the PGA Tour and the LPGA tour. At a major tournament, his Irish face was as much a part of the scenery as the trophy, especially at the British Open, an event he had embellished for American golfers in 1946 when he persuaded Sam Snead to enter. Snead won. Two decades later he persuaded Tony Lema to enter the 1964 British Open at St. Andrews where Tony himself wrote the real afterword for his book. He had arrived after an overnight flight from the PGA Tour event at Whitemarsh in Philadelphia where he had played poorly. But in recent weeks he had won the Thunderbird Classic, the Buick Open and the Cleveland Open as well as the Crosby National Pro-Am earlier in the year. During the overnight flight to Scotland, Corcoran tried to explain the subtleties of the Old Course to him.*

*"I don't build golf courses," Lema said. "I play 'em."*

*His first day there he had time to play only 10 holes before he settled into a rented home he shared with Doug Sanders that week. The next day he played the full 18 holes. His caddie was Tip Anderson, who had helped Arnold Palmer win the British Open in both 1961 and 1962, but in 1964 Palmer had to withdraw. After that practice round, Anderson was asked what he thought of Lema's game.*

*"He'll do," the caddie said.*

*Anderson knew that a newcomer to the British Open, much less a newcomer to St. Andrews, was in for a learning experience. "Allowance must always be made," Bernard Darwin once wrote, "for the strangeness of a strange land. When Bobby Jones first played in our championship he tore up his card and drove his ball out to sea; when Walter Hagen first played he finished in something like the fifty-fifth place. It is hard work to play a game in the other fellow's country, and it seems that a probationary visit is needed before even the greatest can give of their best." But for Tony Lema, a probationary visit would not be needed. He had the swing. He also had the smile and the style. Waiting to tee off in the opening round, he noticed a coin in the grass. He picked it up and flashed it to the gallery.*

*"Look at this," he said, "I'm already the leading money-winner in the British Open."*

*He had the Scots laughing, but he also charmed them with his golf. He shot 73-68-68-70, winning by five strokes over Nicklaus, who would not win his first British Open until two years later. Lema won with a black-painted putter that had been a present from Tommy Armour, a Scottish-born winner of both the United States Open and the British Open more than three decades earlier. And he won by listening to his caddie's advice to use bump-and-run approach shots.*

*"He's a great player," Tip Anderson said. "His swing is about as sweet as Sam Snead's. When you compare his game to Mr. Palmer's, there's very little difference. But he is more relaxed. When something goes wrong, like the 6 he took at the fifth hole Friday, he forgets it immediately."*

*On the final day Lema strung together five consecutive 3's on "The Loop" of the Old Course where the outgoing nine turns into the incoming nine. And when Lema strode off the 18th green next to the Royal & Ancient clubhouse, the Scots were nudging each other, remembering that Lema had predicted he would win. On his arrival he had collaborated on a first-person article for a Scottish newspaper, but when it appeared, the headline shocked him.*

*"I'll Win The Open," it blared.*

*Lema hurried to find Corcoran, who had approved the article but had not been consulted on the headline.*

*"I never said that," Lema said.*

*"You have now," Corcoran said.*

*Lema justified that headline in the first tournament he ever played with the smaller British ball then optional in the British Open. When he arrived in the press tent, he popped the cork on the first of several bottles of champagne that the golf writers would consume. The cork bounced under a table, but Dick Taylor of Golf World magazine crawled to retrieve it. That cork remains one of Taylor's prized mementoes. But halfway through the tournament, Lema had sprung for an impromptu champagne party in the press tent.*

*"What's this party for?" somebody asked.*

*"I'm the 36-hole leader," Lema said.*

*At that stage of his career, he didn't pay for champagne. In a deal that Corcoran had arranged, Lema was supplied by Moet Chandon, even at a casual dinner. He simply signed the tab, which then was dispatched to the Moet Chandon offices. But he didn't drink champagne only when he could sign for it. When he went to Paris to celebrate his British Open victory, he discovered the more expensive French champagne.*

*"We don't get that free," Corcoran said.*

*"Then we'll pay for it," Lema replied.*

*He could afford it. In his last four full years on the PGA Tour, he earned $291,281, a substantial sum in that era dominated by Nicklaus and Palmer. In 1965 his $101,817 ranked second to Nicklaus; in each of the two previous years he had finished fourth on the money list. And in his 11 years on the PGA Tour, he won 13 tournaments, a total that doesn't include his British Open victory. He also was a member of the winning 1965 United States Ryder Cup team. But he once put his finances in perspective.*

*"I'm third in earnings," he said. "And first in spendings."*

*If he were alive today, he surely would be one of the most popular and most successful golfers on the Senior PGA Tour, but he died too early and too tragically. The day after the 1966 PGA Championship in Akron, Ohio, he was to have appeared in Chicago at a one-day exhibition. But on a chartered flight from Akron to Chicago, the small plane crashed and burned on a golf course, between the green and the pond of the 165-yard seventh hole at The Sportsman's Club in Lansing, Ill. Tony, his wife Betty, and the two pilots perished in the blaze.*

*More than two decades later, Tony Lema lives not only in the memories of those golfers who knew him, but also in the memories of those who walked in his galleries. In a letter to* Golf Digest *magazine a few years ago, one of those spectators, Bill Roland, remembered Lema teeing off the final hole of the 1966 PGA Championship at the Firestone Country Club.*

*"He absolutely crushed a drive down the right side of the fairway," Roland wrote. "Next to me, two young boys, about 10 years old, began arguing about who would own the golden tee that Tony had just used and that had landed at their feet. 'Hold on boys,' Tony said. He calmly reached into his pocket and slowly dropped about a dozen golden tees into the outstretched hands of the youngsters, who reacted as if the tees were solid gold.*

*"I couldn't help saying, 'That was nice, Tony.' 'Hey,' he said, smiling toward me, 'they're only kids. Besides, this is my last hole.'*

*"With his head held high, he strolled down the fairway. Little did he know just how special that gesture was to those two youngsters. Little did he know it was his last fairway."*

*In a few hours Tony Lema would be dead. But he had walked his last fairway with the smile and the style that made him special. And that makes "Golfers' Gold" special.*

*Dave Anderson*